# Music, Talent, and Performance
## A CONSERVATORY CULTURAL SYSTEM

D1546178

# MUSIC, TALENT,
## AND
# PERFORMANCE

## A CONSERVATORY CULTURAL SYSTEM

Henry Kingsbury

Temple University Press
Philadelphia

Temple University Press, Philadelphia 19122
Copyright © 1988 by Temple University. All rights reserved
Published 1988
Printed in the United States of America

*Library of Congress Cataloging-in-Publication Data*
Kingsbury, Henry, 1943–
Music, talent, and performance.
1. Ethnomusicology.
2. Music—Instruction and study.
I. Title.
ML3798.K56   1988        781.7        87-10092
ISBN 0-87722-516-8 (alk. paper)

This book is dedicated
with gratitude
to
Nan and Ted
Kingsbury
of
Kennebunk, Maine—
they are peace-seeking folks,
and
wonderful parents

To elucidate the fashion in which music is a patterning based on the attributes of tone . . . would not bring us very close to our object of study; for how this patterning is produced, whether by personal, social, or historical forces, how it is thought of, whether as a language or a mathematical exercise, whether of the feelings or the reason, are all so much of the essence of music that to leave such considerations out of account must be to miss almost everything of philosophic importance. EDWARD A. LIPPMAN, in
*A Humanistic Philosophy of Music*

I do not claim that this answer contains the whole truth about the changing ideals of natural beauty. But I do think the study of the metaphysics of art should always be supplemented by an analysis of its practice, notably the practice of teaching. E. H. GOMBRICH, in
*Art and Illusion*

# CONTENTS

# ACKNOWLEDGMENTS

One of the goals of this book is to call attention to the social and collective nature of things often taken as individualistic, and perhaps because of this I am acutely aware of the fact that there is little of significance in what follows of which I am the sole "author." As one of my former teachers liked to tease, "there is no originality—only ignorance of sources." I am both glad and sorry that there are altogether too many people who have made important contributions to this study for me to enumerate all of them.

No ethnography can ever be written without incurring a deep and complex debt to the community of people who constitute the locus of study. It is not enough simply to say that I will always be grateful to the people of the Eastern Metropolitan Conservatory, although this is certainly the case. During my research there I was given what can only be called kid-glove treatment, and to some of them it may seem ungrateful that I should have written a rather secular account of something that many in the conservatory experience as sacred indeed. My research period at the conservatory enriched my appreciation of music and musicians far more than I can say.

Preparation for this study began in the context of my study of anthropology and ethnomusicology at Indiana University under the tutelage of the late Alan P. Merriam. It was Merriam's enthusiasm that first led me to the study of anthropology, and his well-known desire to integrate the study of music with the study of culture is a seed which I have tried to nurture in this book. His untimely death was a severe blow to me and my work, and many of the shortcomings of what follows can be laid to the fact of their never having been submitted to his review.

Anthropological ethnomusicology has long been an article of faith at Indiana University, but in the aftermath of Dr. Merriam's death it took on the tone of a moral cause. In trying to simultaneously transcend and assimilate the sudden absence of a prominent scholar, the ethnomusicology community in Bloomington generated a spate of restless intellectual and politico-academic activity which to this day continues to affect my thinking. Lively discussions with teachers such as Ronald Smith and Ruth Stone were the locus of some of the first ideas of what is now this book, as were numerous sessions with Jane Cowan, Pam Feldman, William Graves, Carol Inman, Robert Reed, Roberta Singer, Jay Szklut, Sue Tuohy, and many others.

Professors William Corsaro, Michael Herzfeld, Ivan Karp, and Anthony Seeger nursed me—and this work—through the dissertation stage, providing critical and evaluative commentary which would give the lie to any stereotype that may remain of the dissertation committee as gatekeepers of the ivory tower. Adapting the dissertation has proved a more complex task than I could have anticipated, but one of the more pleasant contexts for reworking my analysis were in sessions sponsored by the Northeast Chapter of the Society for Ethnomusicology, and in particular in discussions there with Gregory Gargarian, Janice Kleeman, Jeff Titon, and the late James Koetting. Robert Hefner gave attentive readings to the book at several stages; his suggestions have been of tremendous help. Charles Keil, who had provided so many helpful suggestions at the beginning of my research, also in later stages provided valuable guidance in approaching the world of publishing. There were editorial suggestions from Daniel Goodwin, Judith McCulloh, and Mary Wyer, and helpful discussions with Susan Bruce, Steve Gallant, Lisa Henderson, William Merrill, Sutti Ortiz, Kathleen Schubert, and Anne Sullivan. The entire manuscript got a helpful reading from John Messenger as well as from various anonymous readers in the course of publication review, and Steven Feld came along at just the right time with some trenchant observations regarding the book's organization. For obvious reasons, I also feel indebted to the highly professional staff at Temple University Press.

To William Carroll I owe a very special debt of gratitude for all manner of personal and professional support. That he read and made cogent comments on the manuscript is but the least of it; his administrative support and his patient, quiet encouragement are major reasons this book has come into being.

Finally, the encouragement of Karol Borys has been of incalculable help in completing this undertaking. I suspect that she has learned a good deal from seeing me wrestle my thoughts into presentable form; I know that she has taught me a lot along the way.

# Music, Talent, and Performance
## A CONSERVATORY CULTURAL SYSTEM

# SOCIAL CONTEXT AND ABSOLUTE MUSIC

## An Introduction

From 1969 to 1971, when so many American campuses were embroiled in student unrest over the war that was raging in Southeast Asia, I was a piano teacher and Assistant Dean of the College of Music at Midland University.[1] One of my primary duties was academic counseling—advising students on matters of selecting or changing their major area, counseling students who were in some danger of academic probation, discussing such topics as postgraduate plans, problems of adjusting to the social and academic environment of a music school, and the like. Through this experience, I became increasingly concerned with the importance that music and music making played in the personal lives of these young adults, and I was compelled to focus increasingly on these matters in the consideration of higher musical education.

For many students, there was a great deal of ambivalence, concern, and social or personal tension relating their musicality to their most elemental sense of self and identity. A striking example of this was a young piano student who, halfway through her freshman year, came into my office to discuss some of her difficulties in adjusting to the musical and social ambiance of the College of Music. From the admissions officers as well as from members of the piano faculty I had heard that she was one of the most promising students in her class, and yet she herself was having great misgivings about being a piano student. Toward the end of a rather lengthy and diffuse discussion of her feelings about the College of Music, she mentioned that she had been quite enthralled with a course she was then taking on Japanese culture. "But," she said, "of course I couldn't major in something like that." When I asked her, "Why not?" she answered, in a remarkably innocent way, "Oh, because I'm talented." I suggested to her that she need not experience her own musical talent as an albatross strung around her neck. The next day she was back in my office, saying that it had never before occurred to her to think of her own musical talent in such a way. She had always felt that if she should go into any academic field other than music, it would not only upset her hometown piano teacher and guidance counselor, but more than that, it would devastate her parents, who took great pride in her musical gifts and accomplishments. My memory went back to a few years earlier when one of my own conservatory classmates joked that his mother had stood over him with a baseball bat when he was a child, to enforce disciplined piano practising.

Many music students had been admitted to Midland on the strength of their virtuosity in, say, violin, only to confront for the first time the complicated—and, in the context of the curriculum at the College of Music, absolutely basic and essential—matters of four-part written "harmonic dictation" and the playing of harmonic progressions at the keyboard. One young soprano, presumably equipped with an exemplary singing voice (or in musicians' parlance, a "good instrument"), confessed to me with a definite element of horror that she could not read music written in the bass clef. One might, of course, be tempted to ask how such people could get into a music school in the first place but the fact is that admission to a music school is generally awarded specifically to a high level of skill in a narrowly specified area. The important point for me, however, was the intensity of some students' concern for their identity, engendered by the new set of expectations they found upon entering the College of Music.

Clearly, the social environment was rather unpleasant for some of these people; the College of Music was an environment in which their musical "talent," which had in their childhood been a mark of their remarkable individuality, suddenly became a mark of similarity with all the other students. In such a context, some students inevitably came to entertain doubts as to whether they "really" had talent at all. Such feelings, moreover, were manifested in a complex weave of intensely ambiguous friendly-competitive social relationships. Of course, networks of such relationships constituted fertile ground for the negotiation of conservatory "politics." It was in this light that, in one of the first meetings that I attended of the various Midland University administrators, the Dean of the liberal arts division observed that "of course, in the College of Music they learn more about politics than they do about music." That dean had previously been a professor of political science.

Partly because my own academic training had been in piano performance and not, for example, in educational psychology or some related discipline, the impact of my counseling experience was to impress me with the difference of orientation there can be between the teaching of music and the nurturing of musicality. I came to view musicality as a "drive" rather like sex: certainly the association in many music students between their musicality and their self-image was not unlike the link between a teenager's self-confidence and sense of sexual attractiveness. To me it seemed equally certain that music curricula centered on highly disciplined approaches to musical "technique," formalistic studies in "music theory" omitted far more of the social and personal experience of music and music making than could be adequately dealt with in my own rather haphazard "counseling."

The interplay between music and musicality is an important theme of this book, and many of the problems studied here first presented themselves to me in the context of my experience as a counselor for music students. However, there is a second incident—or rather, pair of incidents—from my career as a music educator and administrator that gave rise to the questions that have energized the present study. These incidents challenged my own conceptions of "absolute" music, of music as something that exists on its own terms, having its own meaning, quite independent of the vagaries of mundane social life.

In the fall of 1969, the Student Mobilization to End the War organization planned a series of nationwide strikes, the first scheduled for October 15, to protest the American war in Indochina. A few weeks before the October 15 date, some of the administrators at Midland were discussing ways of demonstrating "official" concern about the war to an increasingly distressed and turbulent student body. The feeling expressed was that the time had certainly come when students should see that university administrators sympathized with the students in their restiveness, and in at least some way shared their concerns regarding the war.

Someone suggested that the College of Music sponsor a concert for peace on the night of the demonstrations, and I was asked to discuss this possibility with Dean of Music Trevor Waterhouse. When I presented this suggestion to the Dean a few days later, he hesitated, but then told me that he would not allow such a concert to take place, explaining that when music is performed as part of a political protest, its purity is destroyed and its meaning undermined. Music, he said, must not be affixed to any specific political cause. At the time, my personal dismay was checked, albeit feebly, by my musician's intuition that Trevor was speaking from an unassailable position: classical music is a pure and autonomous art form (after all, it is sometimes referred to as "absolute music"[2]) whose true meaning and beauty lie outside the sphere of social life or political tensions.

Seven months later, Midland University was one of the many American colleges and universities to suspend its academic operations in the aftermath of the massacre at Kent State University. During this period there was a veritable spate of student political activism, but at Midland the unquestioned consummation of these activities was two performances by a Midland chorus and orchestra of the Mozart *Requiem*, once on the Midland campus and once in Washington, D.C. The idea originated in a general meeting of the students of the College of Music: why, they asked, didn't the College organize a performance of the *Requiem* in protest against the deaths in Vietnam and Ohio? The suggestion received spontaneous and general enthusiasm. Dean Waterhouse, who was revered in the College of Music as a distinguished and charismatic choral musician (the students knew nothing of his views of politics in music), was the obvious choice for a conductor of this performance. He accepted the students' invitation to lead a performance of the *Requiem*, and for the next few weeks led intensive rehearsals of the chorus and orchestra, culminating in the two public performances. The entire period was one of high emotions, and a rush of enthusiasm could be sensed throughout the College of Music.

The experience of the Mozart *Requiem* forced me, however, into an intense quandary regarding the rejoinder that Trevor Waterhouse had given me a few months earlier. If he really believed that music was a "pure" art that should not be associated with a particular political cause, then why did he agree to lead the *Requiem*? If, as everyone participating seemed clearly to perceive, his involvement in the *Requiem* was complete, was this not in spite of the fact that it was on behalf of a political cause and because of the fact that the *Requiem* was a classic item of the choral repertoire? Was the performance truly a protest against the war and the Kent State massacre, or had the carnage of Vietnam and Kent State become a metaphorical pedestal on which the "pure" beauty of Mozart's masterpiece would be heightened? What was the meaning of the actual music in this case? Indeed, what or where was "the actual music," in the pure, absolute sense that Waterhouse himself had articulated? Could there be any such truly pure music in such a situation, or indeed at any time?

This incident loosened the metaphorical earth around the roots of my own intuition that "classical" music is indeed absolute and in some sense pure, existing in its own right and on its own terms. Although for a while I struggled to resist it, I was eventually unable to avoid the general conclusion that music "itself" is no less but also no more than what people make it and make of it. The contradictions of Trevor Waterhouse and the overwhelming power of the performance of the Mozart *Requiem* unraveled for me the notion of "absolute" music in which I had been trained.

A little over a year later, I left Midland University in a spirit of confusion regarding both the musical and educational work I had been doing and its pertinence to the cultural and political upheaval that was taking place in connection with the war in Asia. About this time, I read Ben Sidran's *Black Talk* (1971) (provocatively subtitled *How the Music of Black America Created a Radical Alternative to the Values of Western Literary Tradition*), a book that made a very strong impression on me for the fairly simple reason that it presented an analysis of Afro-American music which argued the character of the music to be inextricably linked to the cultural history of American blacks. Not surprisingly, a reviewer's quotation printed on the book jacket claimed that Sidran's study presented "a totally new way of looking at black culture in America." To me, however, Sidran's book implicitly suggested a "totally new way" of approaching what I considered to be "my" music, that is, Western "classical" music: if the music of black America took its character and meaning from the cultural fabric of American blacks, didn't that imply that "classical" music—so-called "absolute" music—drew its meaning and character from the sociocultural ambiance of middle-class white America and perhaps Europe?

Such a chain of events led me to view music as a metaphor of the society in which it takes place, a perspective that I have subsequently learned is similar to what ethnomusicologists refer to as the study of "music as culture" (Merriam 1977: 204, Herndon and McLeod 1979). Of course, the field of ethnomusicology has traditionally been associated almost exclusively with non-Western musical idioms, so much so that this non-Western orientation has been central to many scholarly conceptions of the very word "ethnomusicology." (For an historical collection of such conceptions, see Merriam 1977.) More recently, ethnomusicologists have shown interest in applying ethnomusicological principles—particularly those involving the study of music in its cultural context—to Western as well as non-Western music. I suspect that few present-day scholars, for example, would subscribe categorically to Bruno Nettl's early definition of ethnomusicology as "the science that deals with the music of peoples outside of Western civilization" (Nettl 1956: 1). On the other hand, the acceptance of the possibility of applying ethnomusicological principles to the study of Western art music has not entailed its practise, a fact noted in Nettl's more recent observation that "the definition of ethnomusicology as the study of non-Western and folk music, although widely criticized, is descriptively correct" (Nettl 1983: 4).

Thus it was with an eye to putting the shoe on the other foot, as it were, that I began graduate study in ethnomusicology and sociocultural anthropology. Whereas most of the people who take up anthropology do so in order to study the ways of some distant non-Western civilization, I was turning to anthropology in order to deal with issues pertaining to life in what I took to be "my own" culture. The difficulties of starting off in a completely new discipline were considerable. When I began my study of anthropology, the only prominent anthropologists I could name were Margaret Mead and Claude Lévi-Strauss. (As an undergraduate I had read *Magic, Science, and Religion*, but I did not realize that its author, Bronislaw Malinowski, was an anthropologist; since I had read him in a religion course, I presumed he was a scholar of religion!) I might well have been utterly overwhelmed by the entire experience, but for the fact that in the first term of my study I read Edmund Leach's *Political Systems of Highland Burma* (1977), a book that not only gave me my first experience of what anthropologists call "elegance" of analysis, but also presented a particularly unforgettable proposition:

With every kind of technical action, there is always the element which is functionally essential, and another element which is simply the local custom, an aesthetic frill. Such aesthetic frills were referred to by Malinowski as "neutral custom," and in his scheme of functional analysis they are treated as minor irrelevancies. It seems to me, however, that it is precisely these customary frills which provide the social anthropologist with his primary data. Logically, aesthetics and ethics are identical. If we are to understand the ethical rules of a society, it is aesthetics that we must study. (Leach 1977: 12)

Leach's equation of ethics and esthetics was a revolutionary right idea in the right place at the right time. For me the thought that ethics, in the broadest sense of the word—collective values bearing on the dealings of people as they interact with other people—was inextricably linked to esthetics—collective values as they bear on created formal structures or objects—was a major breakthrough. Such a formulation presented a succinct model for bringing together my experiences at Midland—Trevor Waterhouse and the *Requiem*, the supposed "purity" of classical music, the profound connection between the musicality and the self-identity of the music students—and the idea sparked in me by Sidran's book, that musical values must be understood as emanations of social and cultural processes.

# Music and Anthropology

The discipline of anthropology is at least somewhat in advance of its cousin, ethnomusicology, in regard to the study of contemporary Western cultural idioms and social issues. (For an overview of anthropological studies of American culture, see Spindler and Spindler 1983.) Nevertheless, one of the standard textbooks for graduate and undergraduate anthropology classes is entitled *Other Cultures* (Beattie 1964), and a preponderance of anthropological theory and method maintains this traditional orientation toward cultural other-ness. Prominent in the anthropological literature have been books whose titles simply name a particular people (*The Andaman Islanders, The Nuer, The Tiv of Central Nigeria*), others whose titles take the form of characterizing epithets (*The Harmless People, The Forest People*), and others whose titles specify a domain within a particular culture (*Navaho Witchcraft, Nuer Religion*). Underlying much of this literature is an implicit conception of "cultures" as boundable entities (*The Nuer, The Tiv*). The association of anthropology with portrayals of "primitive" societies frequently entails the characterization of a social organization in static equilibrium, presented in the rhetoric of an omniscient "ethnographic present" tense (*The* Nuer *do* thus-and-so).

Although the rhetoric of static equilibrium has become somewhat less prevalent among present-day anthropologists, one of the simplest ways to lend an anthropological aura to studies of modern American culture is to refer to the tradition of studying "simple" or "primitive" societies. For example, J. M. Weatherford entitled his ethnography of the U.S. Congress *Tribes on the Hill* and peppered his account with comparisons of congressmen with "shamans," "bigmen," "warlords," and the like. Weatherford likened newly elected congressional representatives to age-set initiates among the Shavante, a horticultural tribe who live in Brazil: "Just as Shavante men are always known by the name of the cohort with whom they spent their formative years in the bachelor hut, congressmen are always known by the name of the cohort with whom they spent their formative years in the Longworth Building" (Weatherford 1981: 30). Such an association of anthropology with "tribal" peoples, of course, extends well beyond the community of professional anthropologists. For example, I was recently introduced to a conference of musicologists, quite without prompting from me, as "an anthropologist who has studied a conservatory as a tribe." Similarly, one of the secretaries in the conservatory, when informed that I was an anthropologist making a study of the conservatory, exclaimed with both mirth and embarrassment, "Oh, so *we've* become the savages now!"

In light of this state of affairs, I would begin this book by postulating the idea of cultural otherness as centrally important and yet fundamentally problematic and unsettled. Certainly I do not perceive, nor do I want to represent, conservatory musicians as "exotic," "savage," "primitive," or "tribal." On the contrary, a fundamental starting point for the present study is the fact that I myself was trained in several music conservatories and later went on to teach in one; because of my personal and professional background, conservatory culture is very familiar to me. Nevertheless, conservatory culture is also something from which I now feel some distance—the world of a conservatory is in a sense no longer "my" world. Perhaps more precisely, conservatory culture is in different senses both "mine" and "not mine." Thus for my part, I would suggest that the question of whether the people of the Eastern Metropolitan Conservatory—or the U.S. Congress, or, indeed, the Nuer—are ultimately more "us" than "them" is more a humanistic than a scientific question, one more one of attitude than, say, of taxonomic classification.

The problematic, unsettled nature of cultural otherness is nicely exemplified by the phenomenon of musical "talent." On the one hand, people who have musical talent are perceived by many as something of a breed apart, fully appropriate for discussion as an "other" group. On the other hand, one of the fundamental characteristics of musical talent is the indefinite gradations in which it is manifested. I suspect, for example, that some who read this book are likely to feel that they have a certain amount of musical talent, yet not enough to gain admission to a conservatory, and there are certainly some who gain admission to the conservatory who nevertheless continue to harbor uneasy questions about whether their talent is such that they truly belong there. The problem of how much talent it takes to be "really" talented is constantly at issue, and will forever confound efforts to achieve consensus regarding the makeup of any group of "talented" people.

Moreover, although it may seem only common sense to say that "self" and "other" (or "us" and "them") are fundamentally opposed, musical talent confounds, in at least one sense, the experience of "other" with that of "self." In the context of everyday life, to be identified as talented is frequently to be identified as different, and a talented person's knowledge that "I am different" is at least sometimes congruent with the feeling that I (self) am one of them (other). In the context of the conservatory, however, where it is the norm—perhaps more precisely, the expectation—to be talented, the reverse is likely to be the case.

Of course, "exotic" cultures hardly constitute the sole focus of anthropological study, and some of the best recent ethnographies have been studies of educational institutions—some of these by anthropologists, probably more by sociologists. In this connection, it is perhaps worth noting that this book is at least somewhat anomalous regarding the ethnography genre, at least in what some would call its "realist" phase (Marcus and Cushman 1982: 29). In saying this, I mean only that I will not attempt to "sketch vividly . . . the boundaries of a cultural unit" (Marcus 1980: 509). The present book is not intended as a narrative portrayal of the Eastern Metropolitan Conservatory of Music, as an ethnography, in a technical sense, of an educational institution.

On the other hand, a significant distinction was made by Clifford Geertz when he noted that "the locus of study is not the object of study. Anthropologists don't study villages (tribes, towns, neighborhoods . . . ); they study *in* villages" (Geertz 1973: 22, emphasis in original). In light of this distinction, it can be said that this book is indeed based on ethnographic research, not so much *of* a conservatory (although one chapter will be devoted to the dynamics of the conservatory institution) as *in* a conservatory. This study is ethnographic in the sense that it draws on what social scientists call "participant observation" research, that day-by-day process of watching, listening, asking, interviewing, recording and note taking that constitutes the production of "data." It is in this sense that this work is presented as ethnography, although less as an ethnography of a conservatory than as an ethnography of music.

This book deals with music not as a nicely bounded "cultural unit," but rather with an open-ended framework of cultural concepts and social configurations. The succeeding chapters deal with various contexts in which music is produced, experienced, and evaluated, with a concluding chapter suggesting a "cultural system" constructed from a consideration of the relationships among and interpenetration of these contexts.

The first of these contexts, that of the conservatory institution, will be discussed in Chapter Two; a main focus of this chapter will be the relationship between the "aural tradition" of Western art music performance and the decentralized "political" organization of the conservatory institution, both of which are centered largely on the school's individual performer-teachers. Chapter Three will discuss a second, cultural, context, namely the concept of "talent," which for the conservatory is a point of both contrast and similarity with the world around it (while a music conservatory might be distinguished as a community of the talented, nevertheless "talent" is at issue not only in music, but also in literature, sports, business, and so on). The starting point for this chapter will be the fact that, although talent is often conceived as something which you either have or you don't, nevertheless, conservatory life—and probably, American life in general—is characterized by disagreements among people regarding whether or not a particular person "really" has talent. The following chapter will discuss a series of "master classes" in chamber music performance, focusing on the importance the teacher placed on playing what the score said to play, and yet not to play simply because the score said so, but rather because one "felt" it that way. As with other musical contexts, the matter of social power is of central importance in the master classes, here particularly in connection with the social authority of the distinguished teacher in evaluating whether or not the students were playing with feeling. Such a judgment is closely related to, if not indeed identical with, an evaluation of talent. Chapter Five will analyze the context of formal solo recitals, presented here as rituals in what Emile Durkheim called the "cult of the individual," rituals in which the social separation between the soloist and the audience is, in an important sense, sacralized.

The concluding chapter draws on materials from the previous chapters as well as from writings in the musicological and social science literature in putting forth an anthropological conception of music as a polymorphic cultural reality. Such a conception draws on the variety of representations of what music "really" is, and on an interpretation of this variation in terms of social configurations in and around the conservatory. The point is that notions of "music" in the conservatory are varied and divergent—no single meaning of the word applies in all cases—and yet these varied conceptualizations of music are also mutually interdependent. Music is presented here as a cultural integument of social process (Leach's equating of ethics and aesthetics, mentioned earlier, is directly to the point), the cultural garb of interaction among conservatory persons. Although musicians conceive of "music" as being intrinsically extrasocial, many of their most intensely spoken references to "the actual music" are unambiguous comments on particular persons in specific social situations.

I hasten to emphasize that the various musical contexts in terms of which this book is organized are neither independent nor discrete domains, nor are they all contexts in the same sense of the term. The concept of *talent*, for example, is a musical *context* in a very different sense from the conservatory institution. It should also be stressed that each of these four contexts entails other contexts (for example, the context of the authoritative pedagogue in the master class also entails the context of the authoritative musical score, or urtext), and that these various contexts contextualize each other. Each is a musical context in the sense that it lends a particular significance and meaning to music.

I would emphasize also that the various contexts which constitute the basis of this book are not intended as either definitive or exhaustive, and the "cultural system" suggested here is just that—a suggestion. For clarification, I would stress the indefinite article in the book's subtitle—*A* Conservatory Cultural System. No claims will be made in this book in terms of *The* Conservatory Cultural System. Nevertheless, I do think that the notion of "cultural system," conceived in terms of intertwined musical contexts, is an optimal, perhaps even ideal, manner of characterizing what music really is, partly because such a notion facilitates a central focus on the variety of the senses of what music is taken to be.

Of course, such an approach will seem anomalous to some, for although it is common enough in musicological books to read that, for example, "music is a product of human activity," such statements are made more often as parenthetical asides than as substantive comments on musicological method. Indeed, many scholars of Western art music believe that musicological inquiry can only be distorted by the introduction of problems of social action, which are characteristically perceived as "extramusical" and hence parasitic on studies of "the actual music." (This is, of course, the musicological equivalent to Dean Waterhouse's original opinion that the purity of great music should not be linked in performance to any specific political cause.) The standard rhetoric for this is that music be studied "on its own terms," a phrase which generally means that certain abstract concepts ("melody," "harmony," "rhythm") are to be analyzed in terms of other similarly abstract terms ("structure," "form," "development"). The prevailing idea is that music is not to be understood in terms of its sociocultural context, but rather in terms of its internal organization and cohesion.

My own view is that such an approach is at bottom a way of taking "music" out of context in order to study it. I am in fundamental agreement with the statement of ethnomusicologist John Blacking: "we must recognize that no musical style has 'its own terms': its terms are the terms of its society and culture" (Blacking 1973: 25). In light of this idea, the value of anthropological "participant observation" in a conservatory of music is precisely that a conservatory is an environment in which musical terms are negotiated, largely in terms of the preceding configuration of musical contexts, with great intensity and on a daily basis. A music conservatory is a place where musical disagreements are continually being negotiated toward consensus, and where consensus is in turn continually breaking up into contention. If the strength of theory, whether scientific, social scientific, or musicological, is linked to the logical possibility of either confirmation or refutation, then anthropological study in a music conservatory might be said to have a privileged position regarding music "theory," in that it takes as its data base that very continuum linking disagreement with consensus in musical discourse.

This book is a study of that musical idiom which more than any other has traditionally been referred to in academic literature simply as "music," with no modifier such as "folk," "popular," "country," or "primitive." It was not too long ago that when one read the newspaper reviews of concerts of "classical" or "serious" music the reviewers could and did claim simply to be writing about "music": the word with no modifier (although sometimes simply called "good" music! see, for example, Salzer 1962: 3–4, or Cone 1968: 13) was taken to conflate a particular repertoire with music *per se*, with music in its essence. I would prefer, however, to characterize this book as a study of a cultural idiom produced by and in a rather specific configuration of social production. This configuration entails (1) the lionized composer (even though the composer is stereotypically not living), (2) the gifted and highly trained performers who render faithful and "felt" interpretations of the composer's sacralized text, and (3) an ostensibly anonymous public audience. The configuration also includes (4) the scholarly musicologists and (5) the journalistic critics who write about this musical idiom. Until recent years, such writers reserved for this idiom the sole claim to the domain of "music."[3] Finally, the configuration is characterized by (6) highly formalized private teacher-student dyads. Such a sixfold configuration, taken as a mode of cultural production, a configuration of collective action, is suggested as a preliminary conceptualization of the present study.[4]

# Entering "the Field"

Anthropologists characteristically refer to participant-observation research as "fieldwork," and it is of at least passing interest to wonder just how much this terminology is linked to the historical fact that anthropology has traditionally been concerned with the study of what until fairly recently were called "tribal," "simple," or "primitive" societies. The study of such societies is often done in an environment quite dramatically different from that including automobiles to go to and from the supermarket, workplace, or cinema, or to huge libraries with microfiche readers and computerized search procedures. Indeed, the matter of getting into "the field" is for some anthropologists reckoned in terms of miles hiked beyond the last access to four-wheel drive vehicles, airlift, or boat landing, as well as in terms of finding—perhaps even making—a place to stay, and adjusting to sometimes dangerous factors concerning nutrition and hygiene.

In view of such factors, it is with considerable hesitancy that I would call my research "fieldwork" or the Eastern Metropolitan Conservatory of Music the "field." EMCM is, as I knew in advance it would probably be, a music school rather like those that I had experienced previously, yet also different in various respects, and its location is nothing particularly more nor less than a typical major American city.

The Eastern Metropolitan Conservatory of Music offers the degrees Bachelor of Music, Bachelor of Music Education, Master of Music, and Artist Diploma. In the specialization of its focus, the conservatory might be compared with schools of law, medicine, or nursing, but its relation to the economy and the world around it is quite different from that of a professional school. For one thing, professions such as law, medicine, and nursing are regulated by governmental licensing agencies, and students in law schools, for instance, are precluded from practising law until after finishing school and obtaining the appropriate license. By contrast, many students come to the conservatory as already developed performing musicians, and conservatory students are frequently engaged at least part-time as wage-earning performers, and have a certain self-image as "professional" musicians. That said, it must also be emphasized that students of law, nursing, or medicine can afford to be much more sanguine regarding professional employment *after* their training than can conservatory students. In contrast with these professional schools, it is only a small minority of conservatory alumni who will be able to go on to a financially life-supporting career in music. In light of this, the paid performing done by conservatory students might be better understood in economic terms as comparable with a summer job rather than as "professional" work. Indeed, the conservatory maintains a "gig office" for the purpose of arranging performing jobs for students in need of financial aid.

With regard to the long-term economic prospects that await conservatory students, Becker's observations (1982: 52ff.) regarding students at various kinds of arts schools are, in all probability, to the point. He points to several studies that indicate that the students and alumni of arts schools participate more as devoted and sophisticated consumers (subscribers to concert or theater series, memberships in museums, and so on) than as performing or economically productive artists. My own research includes only relatively superficial information on this point, and yet my sense is that a conservatory is probably more appropriately compared with a seminary than with a professional school, in that the concentrated focus of conservatory training seems more an inculcation of devotion than a preparation for a career. The sense of commitment among conservatory students seems more personal, moral, and emotional than professional or economic.

My choice of EMCM as an object of research was based mainly on the fact that it is a well-known and highly respected music conservatory, but one with which I had had no direct experience during my own career as a musician. In the summer of 1980, I discussed my plans for research with Stuart Robinson, Director of EMCM. My primary intent at that time was to give Robinson and the EMCM administration ample advance notice of my interest in doing my research in their institution. While I was able only to give him a rather general account of my intended research, his response was largely favorable. When a year later I did send a copy of my research plan to Stuart Robinson, it developed that there were reservations regarding my research at EMCM, mainly due to some administrative changes taking place at that time, not the least of which was Robinson's own imminent departure as Director. I tried to reassure Robinson that I would not create a problem for either him or his successor, that I saw my presence at EMCM as in essence a "mock student," needing no more special attention from the conservatory administrators than any regular conservatory student.

Although Robinson had said that there might be some restrictive "ground rules" pertaining to my visit, I was aware of no such rules when I arrived. Indeed, Robinson referred me to Emeritus Dean Harold Sullivan, who gave me something akin to red-carpet treatment upon my arrival at EMCM. He gave me a guided tour of the premises, as well as lengthy discourses on the conservatory's history and governmental and administrative structures. He also helped me to arrange a schedule of conservatory classes to attend.

My research at EMCM lasted one semester, January–June 1982. I selected four classes to attend on a regular basis. One was a freshman class in "Sight Singing and Ear Training," another was an upper class course entitled "Diction for Singers," and a third was a course in chamber music performance. Dean Sullivan came with me to the first meeting of the classes, introduced me to the teachers, and explained to each that I would be a visitor to the conservatory for the semester, observing classes and rehearsals, and asking if the teacher would object to my presence in the class. The latter question was not simply rhetorical. To one teacher he said, "Now, Andy, if you've already got more than you think you can handle in this class, then you just say so." The closest thing to a negative response was one teacher's comment that he usually did not like to have auditors, but in this instance it would be okay. The fourth class was a "music literature" course dealing with twentieth-century composers. Since this met on a day when Dean Sullivan was not at the conservatory, I introduced myself to the teacher of this class, and asked if I might sit in on it. He too was agreeable to the request.

Particularly in the first weeks of my stay at EMCM, I spent a considerable amount of time chatting with the three secretaries in the outer reception area of the Director's office. It is, of course, a widely accepted element of academic folklore that departmental secretaries are generally repositories of extensive knowledge of the ways of the department they work for, and I have no doubt that these women fit this stereotype as well as any. One of them, Ellen MacDowell, was the special administrative assistant to Stuart Robinson, and would occasionally claim—in a way that was both in jest and in earnest—that she was an administrator and not really "just" a secretary. In saying this she may have been simply making a comment on her somewhat superior rank in relation to the other secretaries, but the correctness of her assertion is argued also by the fact that by midsemester her own dismissal had been effectively attached to Robinson's. Another secretary, Margaret Arnold, was also a part-time student finishing a graduate degree in the conservatory. Margaret was the only trained musician among the secretaries, but it should be emphasized that all of these women were and felt themselves to be very much involved with the conservatory. As Ellen once said, "Those of us who don't have the talent or the creativity can still be creative in nurturing musical talent—

and I think that's important."[5] Ellen had, in fact, previously worked in a theological seminary; she told me that she had thought that working in the conservatory would be a move into the secular world, but she had come to feel that there was much in common between conservatory and seminary life.

In addition to the four classes I attended regularly, I also sat in on occasional master classes given by visiting artists, and many rehearsals of choral, orchestral, and smaller chamber music groups, when these rehearsals were held in large rehearsal halls where I could watch unobtrusively if not unobserved. My original hope had been to make a fairly intensive longitudinal study of rehearsals, in an effort to learn about what changes are made over time in the way a piece gets played, and how these changes—"improvements"—are negotiated within the group. I was unable to do this, due partly to the complications of the rehearsal schedules of the larger groups, and partly to the self-consciousness and consternation which greeted my requests to visit rehearsals of student trios and quartets. Similarly, I was unable to organize my intended project of interviews and rehearsal observations of students preparing degree recitals, for reasons that were partly bureaucratic (the conservatory had no reliable student directory) and partly emotional: numerous students declined to be interviewed until after their recital was over. I did, however, do about two dozen "formal" interviews, that is, interviews set by appointment, with a prepared list of questions, and usually with an audio tape recorder going. Many of these interviews were with seniors and graduate students who had recently performed their degree recital and were approaching the end of their stay at EMCM.

For two interrelated reasons, the heading "entering the field" could appropriately be applied to the entire duration of my stay at EMCM. First, my visit was so brief that even when it was coming to an end, I was not only still meeting new people, but also learning some seemingly basic things about the institution, such as where and when the opera rehearsals took place, or the fact that the piano department had regular weekly master classes in the smaller recital hall of the conservatory. Second, as a visiting researcher in the conservatory I experienced considerable and continual difficulties regarding my own self-presentation. I sensed a feeling of dishonesty in simply describing myself as an anthropologist, as a graduate student preparing my doctoral dissertation, or some similarly nonmusical category, without also saying something about my earlier career as a professional classical musician. On the other hand, I thought it would be confusing to have begun introducing myself as a former dean at the Midland College of Music. Generally, I presented myself as an anthropology graduate student doing research in and about the conservatory; as the conversation led to matters where my own musical background was obviously pertinent or relevant, I would then mention that I had been a musician.

My participation in the sight-singing and ear-training class provides an example of one aspect of this latter problem. This is a class in which the basic mode of teaching is neither lecture nor class discussion, but rather consists of class singing from a book of musical exercises. This is something in which my own skills were considerably greater than those of the students in the class, and in a context such as this where the less confident students tend to take cues from others perceived as more skilled, I had to weigh the relative risks of skewing the progress of the lesson at hand, or making myself more conspicuous by virtue of my own nonparticipation. I decided that the optimal mix of honesty and research efficacy was to use these drills as a means of renewing my own sight-singing skills and to sing with the class, but deliberately to sing semiaudibly, thus minimizing my "contribution" to the performance by the rest of the class.

My sensitivity about being perceived as an "observer" was heightened considerably in the first week of classes. A student who, as it happened, saw me introduced by Dean Sullivan to two different faculty members cheerily asked me if I were a new student in the school. I answered to the effect that I was "sort of" a new student, that in fact I was a student from another university visiting the conservatory for a semester as a participant observer, working toward my doctoral dissertation. When I saw her a few days later this student answered my greeting with an "Oh, hi, how's your *observing* going?" in a way that indicated that she was considerably less than enthusiastic about being a possible object of inquiry.

Nevertheless, there can be little question that it was primarily as an observer that I experienced EMCM. One reason is that, although this was the first time I had ever dealt with EMCM, conservatory life in general is something about which I had made some important career decisions a decade earlier, decisions that were grounded in some emotionally charged experiences from my own conservatory life. There was much in my visit to EMCM that was of a *deja vu* nature (for example, two of my onetime colleagues at Midland were now part-time members of the EMCM faculty). My adoption of an "observer" stance during my research can be understood at least in part as a strategy for modulating my own sense of self with my research aims.

I tried to observe every social interaction in terms of the question, "What is at issue here?" to see what was being negotiated, decided, clarified, altered, maintained—what was in contention, in doubt. There can be little doubt that such a strategy on my part tended to inhibit still further my willingness and ability to "join" the conservatory community, confining my role in most situations to that of spectator rather than participant. Occasionally I would ask someone about what had just happened in a particular interaction, in the hope of complementing my own perceptions with those of the protagonists in the event in question. Ideally this kind of questioning not only generates new information but also serves as a check against premature or biased inference by the researcher. On the other hand, since the events for which such direct questioning was most desirable were frequently interactions with a significant quotient of conflict between the participants, the very act of questioning was sometimes problematic for my relationship with the person in question. Such questioning did, occasionally, result in some embarrassment for me and apparently for some "informants." On this matter I was certainly at least somewhat guilty of the "once bitten, twice shy" syndrome, and I eventually effected a strategy of eliciting elaborations and clarifications, or of cross-checking my own inferences only with particular persons with whom I had established a relationship of a certain degree of solidarity, even if or when they were not directly involved in the particular event at issue.

A methodological point should be made regarding my "what is at issue" guideline question, particularly in connection with the preceding discussion of ethnography as based on observed "data." "What is at issue?" is an analytical question, and any answer to such a question must be viewed at least in part as interpretation, or analysis, rather than as "raw" data. It may well be that in ethnography, or in social science generally, there can in fact be no truly "raw" data: my notebooks are filled with my own on-the-spot *analyses* of what was transpiring at the conservatory. Moreover, since it is self-evident that no researcher could possibly document everything that transpired in his or her presence, it should also be obvious that "field notes" are inevitably selections from among the analytic inferences drawn by the observer-researcher, and that these selections are themselves made analytically, in terms of what the researcher perceives at the time to be particularly significant.

However, it was in terms of the "what is at issue?" question that I felt I would be able to make the most efficient use of my own musical knowledge, while at the same time minimizing the extent to which my previous experience might distort my observations in the conservatory. As I observed my conservatory classes I was constantly asking myself, why would X have said that to Y? (i.e., what is at issue for X?). Why should Y have replied in just that way? (what is at issue for Y?). Answers to such questions sometimes came from the progression of the interaction itself (i.e., it would inferentially become clear why X and Y had said what they said), and sometimes from my own direct questioning of X or Y.

Of course, my own professional background in music was a significant factor in my assessing what was said and what was negotiated in a given interaction. On the other hand, my "what is at issue" question did tend to keep me from drawing premature conclusions when teachers or students at the conservatory explained things, as was almost constantly the case, in terms of "the actual music"—comments which were frequently completed with tags such as "you see" or "if you know what I mean." I had to assume that quite possibly I didn't know what they meant, and thus it was my concern for finding out "what is at issue" that led me toward the conclusion—which is a central argument of this book—that the word *music*, rather than having a fixed and generally understood referent in the real world, is highly shifting and indeterminate in meaning.

As was suggested in the opening pages of this chapter, this book deals centrally with the interplay between music and musicality, that is, with the relationship between interpretation of music and the assessment of musicality. This problem can be conceived as having two aspects. First, there are various ways in which musicians understand the relationship between individual and collectivity, and second, there are a variety of ways in which abstractions are made concrete in social practise. The latter aspect of the problem entails describing and accounting for some of the varied senses of the term *music* as they are used in everyday conservatory dialogue. One procedure which I have brought to my analysis is to ask, what are conservatory musicians talking about when they refer to "music," or to "the actual music," or the music "itself"? The answer which my research has forced on me is that very often they are in effect talking about *each other*. This is what I mean by calling music a cultural integument of social action.

# Some Considerations of
# Analytic Adequacy

An anecdote should provide a link between the preceding discussion and an issue of particular analytic significance. One day Andy Marelli, the teacher of my sight-singing class, discussed with me at some length his perception of changes in the conservatory over the past fifteen or so years. He said that the general quality of the students in the conservatory had declined considerably over the years, despite the generally greater technical skills of the students. He agreed with my observation that students were performing increasingly demanding recital programs with remarkable skill and competence; he also volunteered that his theory classes of the present day have greater ability, on the whole, to sing four-part Bach chorales in class than students of a decade ago. But this, he said, has nothing whatsoever to do with the actual performance of music, of putting it across musically.

He made these comments to me in the context of an hour-long discussion, a conversation which I recorded in my notebook from memory when he left for his next class. It was, in fact, a standard note-taking practise for me to go into the library, an empty classroom, or a nearby coffee shop to make notes on conversations and events just passed if, as was fairly often the case, it seemed inappropriate to be taking notes during the interaction. In this case, however, I began my note taking with a strong sense of confusion about what Andy had been trying to explain to me. Whereas in other cases I was able to start my note taking with a general statement of what had transpired, and then proceed to record approximate (and sometimes verbatim) quotations from the interaction, in this instance I had to work from specific phrases and sentences toward a general approximation of what he had been trying to say.

The reason for this confusion relates directly to an important analytic concern. At one point in the conversation I mentioned that for the sake of clarity I wanted to be certain that he and I were using the word *music* in the same sense, and asked him to clarify his usage of the term. The result was like the fable of the millipede who got so tangled up when he tried to explain how he kept all his leg movements coordinated! Andy tried to clarify his point by approaching it from a different perspective, but in so doing made a quite different observation, namely that some students had complained to him that other students were not really interested in music. His answer to my request for clarification led to a feeling that I had misunderstood the entire drift of what he had been trying to say.

It was my request that Andy specify what he meant by the terms "music" and "musical" that transformed a sense of mutual understanding into one of confusion and uncertainty. My own immediate reaction was to regret that I had not captured the conversation on tape, so that I could study in some detail the expressions used by both Andy and me, perhaps asking Andy to listen to the tape as well, to get further elaborations from him regarding particular points he was making or trying to make. Even without this, however, there is an important lesson to be learned from this interaction, one whose application goes well beyond this particular conversation with a particular individual.

Conservatory musicians continually treat the terms "music" and "musical" as *terra firma* categories in their explanatory statements, in spite of the fact that these notions are highly contingent and occasionally self-contradictory. When the contingent or self-contradictory character of the "music" category is pointed out, the response is sometimes characterized less by confusion or consternation than by a form of mystification whereby contradiction is accorded the elevated status of "paradox," and becomes ideologically integrated into the aesthetic or spiritual power of music, "itself."

My request for clarification effectively changed my role in the conversation from that of an "insider" to an "outsider" role. While many (probably most) people in the conservatory would disagree with Andy's position about a trend of declining musical quality of students in the conservatory, no conservatory insider would claim not to understand what he was saying, which is, in essence, what I was implying with my request for clarification. I am certain that Andy, knowing as he did that I was a trained musician, was assuming some specific knowledge on my part, and it was in terms of that assumption that he was explaining the declining quality of conservatory students.

Andy was explaining what he experienced as a rather unambiguous opinion (perhaps he would even have claimed it as a "fact") about the conservatory. The difficulty arose when I asked him to make an implicit category explicit. He responded by (1) admitting that "music" is indeed a nebulous term, but also (2) saying that this did not at all invalidate his claim, and finally (3) "clarifying" his point by making a quite different point. Through this confusion, an important analytic point should be clear: explanatory accounts made to a researcher (such as myself) by "informants" (such as Andy) are contingent upon the "informant's" perception of the researcher.

Here one must confront a crucial question of epistemological adequacy, namely of what it is, if anything, that allows a social scientist to claim knowledge beyond or in any way greater than that of the "informants." Such a concern had a personal meaning for me during my research period, as there was frequently a dilemma of not wanting to appear arrogant yet also not wanting my work to seem obvious or redundant. The faculty member who more than once asked if at the end of my research I would "form an opinion" regarding what I had observed focused this problem for me quite clearly.[6] The difference between my analysis and the explanations made to me by members of the EMCM community can be stated as one of purpose. The "semi-theoretical disposition" (Bourdieu 1977: 18) of a musician discussing social process in the conservatory is linked to the purposes surrounding such a discussion, purposes that in turn are linked to the social dynamics of the conservatory community. The claim of a more genuinely theoretical disposition in an anthropological study such as my own is based largely on its purpose of accounting for conservatory life not only to the members of the conservatory community, but also—and simultaneously—in terms of procedures and analytical categories devised by interpretive social scientists.

The fact that Andy Marelli was unable to give me a succinct definition of what he meant by his use of the terms "music" and "musical" does not in any way diminish the value of the information he gave me—quite the contrary. His inability to clarify his terms for me is important information in itself, and although his comments came in what was ostensibly an "explanation," his usage of the "music" concept was practical and not theoretical, in terms of the distinction made in the preceding paragraph. For the purposes of his dealings in the conservatory, Andy's explanations would have been quite adequate; no uncertainties about his categories would have been experienced by his colleagues.

Although a major goal of my study includes accounting for the sensory experience of social action, the approach taken here is not that of explaining practical and implicit categories of meaning through an intensification or refinement *ad infinitum* of definitions and glossing terms, nor of mediating the levels of consciousness through the coining of terms with which to identify nonverbal experience. As an item of contrast, a clear example of the latter procedure can be seen in David Sudnow's discourse on jazz in *Ways of the Hand* (1978). Sudnow's discussion of "the organization of improvised conduct" does indeed bring him to deal with practical and cultural knowledge, specifically as it informs body movements and sensations. Sudnow's study, however, is based almost entirely on introspective monitoring of his own sensibilities; he presents improvisation as an extension of skills which are gradually but formally learned, and his presentation relies heavily on terms coined for the purpose of describing his own sensations— "wayfully," "melodying," "contextual soundedness," and the like. Sudnow's explanation is of the relations existing among the mind, hand, sounds, and keyboard. Since he is essentially his only informant, social action cannot be said to be a central concern of his study.

By contrast, any answer to my "what is at issue?" question must include the matter of who is interacting with whom, and in turn with the respective social perceptions that each has of the other. Among other things, this means that the present study deals with matters of social power and authority, with actors' perceptions of social power and authority, and with perceptions of differential social knowledge among actors–all of which, of course, are closely related to each other. The point of my discussion with Andy Marelli is that in this study I am dealing with both the explicit and implicit (Douglas 1978) meanings, both the practical and the theoretical (Bourdieu 1977) knowledge of conservatory musicians, by explaining the implicit meanings and practical knowledge as situated in the actions of particular social groups and configurations with particular structures of power and authority. Although Andy used some terms in a way that he could not explicate, he used the terms in the expectation that no explication would be necessary. He did so because he knew that I was a trained musician and music educator, and thus someone who should be able to understand his meaning implicitly. The value of social analysis lies in the fact that such implicit meanings and practical knowledge are grounded in social relations, and that such social relations can, within certain limitations, be made explicit and theoretical.

The problem of analytic adequacy is one of the relation between "us" and "them," or the contrast between actors' models and analysts' models. Such a contrast, however, is more readily maintained in theory than in practise, since even the most energetic social actor is also very much a social analyst, and the most analytic social observer is obviously also a social actor. Indeed, my own confusion in the preceding incident was caused largely by my momentary failure to monitor my shift from insider ("actor") to outsider ("analyst") roles. No social analysis is ever divorced from practical application in the community it studies. Nor, in my opinion, should it be.[7]

# THE CONSERVATORY

## The Setting

If you go to the front door of the conservatory, to the portal with the lintel proclaiming "Eastern Metropolitan Conservatory of Music," you can't get in. Rather, there is a small cardboard sign on the door with an arrow pointing to the left: "PLEASE USE THE NORTH STREET ENTRANCE." The sign is clearly not the work of a professional sign painter, although its letters are square and crisp. Nevertheless, the sign is, or at least for the duration of my visit, was, a permanent fixture of the front entrance. Honoring the detour, one immediately senses that the operational entrance was selected on account of its orientation facing the conservatory's dormitory and cafeteria building on the other side of North Street. Conservatory students wear an often visible crosswalk into the street between the two buildings; this block of North Street seems almost to be part of the conservatory property. Inside the entrance, a security guard checks people for conservatory identification and signs visitors in and out of the building. The social pressures and tensions of modern urban life have made such security precautions necessary, and budgetary limitations in the conservatory have made it unfeasible to keep more than one doorway available for use.

Once inside the building, the continuing impression is that of one-time elegance mixed with present-day thrift. That the building should be an old one is in itself of no particular significance; what is noteworthy about the edifice is the fact that it is neither dilapidated and run down nor renovated and refurbished. There is none of the pathos associated with a once elegant property falling into disrepair, but neither is there any sense of swagger emanating from modern rebuilding. Without being grandiose, the hallways and marble staircases are spacious: there is no sense of the urgent efficiency that one experiences in many newer academic and business buildings. The stairways are large enough to allow one to stop and talk with others on the steps without the usual sense of unbalanced awkwardness.

Here and there one sees literally shining evidence of a tradition of elegance; some magnificent nineteenth-century furnishings in one of the administrative offices, a display case of the same era, full of exotic musical instruments, in a chamber music room that by virtue of its dimensions and decor must be classed as a parlor. At the same time, there are items that may give to some an impression of pseudoelegance, such as the plaster copies of the "Elgin Marbles" which are mounted in some of the building's hallways. In several places one sees displays of autographed photographs of various bygone concert artists, conductors, opera singers, and the like.

In the main foyer there is a bronze casting of Beethoven, standing on a stone pedestal. In terms of sculptural or architectural esthetics, the statue is much too large for the space allocated to it, but the visual esthetics of the statue seem relatively insignificant. The god of nineteenth-century romanticism, Beethoven is in some ways still a god in the conservatory, but the students' experience of Beethoven is a living one, and the "graven image" is treated with familiarity. It is a popular rendezvous point ("I'll meet you by Beethoven at five o'clock, okay?"), and the bronze folds of Beethoven's cape are regularly covered with taped messages—"Stravinsky septet rehearsal in 224E," or "Martha, we're at MacDonalds—S."

The focal point of the conservatory building is its main concert hall, a splendid 1,500 seat auditorium with an arched parquet ceiling and an expansive, handsome wooden concert stage. This hall is the site of almost daily performances by faculty and students, from individual recitals to choral and orchestral concerts, as well as of concerts sponsored by one or another of the metropolitan subscription series. Over and above the visual impact made by the auditorium and by its unusually fine acoustical characteristics, this concert hall is a conscious symbol of the conservatory. In a dress rehearsal on the eve of a public performance, one conductor exhorted his ensemble by saying that "there's a great legacy to this hall, a lot of great musicians have played here. When you walk out on stage tomorrow night you have to reflect all the best qualities of this school." Indeed, I do not think I am pressing my anthropological bias unduly in suggesting that the entire building can be taken as a symbol of the conservatory's own past.

# Principles of Conservatory Social Organization

The Beethoven statue is certainly not the only place where conservatory communication takes the form of handwritten notes. On the doors of the various administrative offices one frequently sees notices such as "Ira Samuels, see the Dean—TODAY!!!" and "All student ID cards must have validation renewed by Friday." To a visitor, such communications might seem to be only in keeping with the thriftiness that is visually evident with regard to the maintenance of the building—after all, felt pen and masking tape are clearly cheaper and quicker than the postal service, and because they are located near the North Street entrance, the administrative offices are *en route* to almost everything in the building.

Such informality of administrative communication, however, is but one aspect of a strikingly decentralized institutional structure in the conservatory. Perhaps not surprisingly, administrative snafus and perceived insensitivities are the object of a sizeable collection of student gripes and anecdotes. "I had been at this school a whole semester before I even knew that I had a mailbox," complained one graduate student, who added, "I missed out on a lot of information because of that . . . and the deal they have at registration. They just hung out sign-up sheets a week before for registration times. Well, I only come in to school three days a week, and by the time I saw those sheets all the earliest times were gone, so of course all the courses I wanted to take had filled long before I got to register. And this is my last year, so I *won't get* to take them."

Although such foibles of institutional communication may be the most prevalent indicators of a decentralized conservatory structure, they are certainly not the only such signs. When a teacher cannot meet a scheduled class, the standard procedure is to cancel the class, notifying the students with a small card posted on the classroom door. Apart from the fact that even this form of communication is sometimes not used (among the classes that I attended, cancellation notices were not displayed on two occasions when a teacher missed a second day in succession), the significant point is that such classes are not taught by replacement teachers.[1] In many cases it would be quite meaningless to suggest that one teacher stand in during another teacher's absence.

This relates to the fact that the primary method of tuition in the conservatory is private lessons in a given instrument or voice. When the music educational environment is that of a one-to-one relationship, having one teacher serve as stand-in for another is not like having a substitute teach a mathematics class, but rather is more like a change of subject matter. This applies as well to the classroom teaching of subjects such as music history or music theory. When the teacher of the freshman music theory class that I was attending missed three weeks of classes due to illness, there was no replacement until the last few days of his absence, when a graduate student met the class. Of course, the fact that there finally was a replacement demonstrates clearly that in such a case the musical persona of the teacher was not the defining characteristic of the course, and given this fact, one might question the institutional commitment to such classes.

I must emphasize that my concern here is not to chide the conservatory administrators for being remiss in their duties, since such complaints only contribute to the body of conservatory griping about supposed administrative ineptitude and insensitivity. My intent, rather, is to contribute an analysis of conservatory social organization, and to do this by setting forth some of the concepts by which the institution is administered (Leach 1977: 4). Behind the griping about administrative matters in the conservatory is an assumption that problems are caused by the actions or inactions of specific individuals and that responsibility lies directly with the individual persons. This idea of individual responsibility, of course, is closely related to what is sometimes colloquially called the "evil man theory," exemplified, for example, by the belief among many American activists in the 1960s that getting Lyndon Johnson out of office was the way to end the war in Indochina. Thus, rather than leaving the analysis of this level, it may be helpful to look a bit deeper for notions, beliefs, or attitudes that are consistent with both the fact that certain individuals act as they do and that others quite regularly complain about it.

The main thesis of my analysis has four aspects. First, the conservatory places a very high premium on the individual artistic quality of its teachers. Second, teachers are frequently nodal points in the organization of conservatory students into cliques, such that the social organization of the conservatory resembles a patron-client system of social organization.[2] Third, the student-cliques along with the individualistic teaching constitute and contribute to the aural tradition of a musical idiom usually characterized as literate. Finally, the value of artistic individualism and the patronage structure that maintains it are in direct conflict with the principles and workings of a bureaucratic administrative structure.

Evidence for the first aspect—the fundamental importance of the faculty artists—comes from various sources. At the commencement exercises at the end of my stay at the conservatory, the chairman of the board of trustees began his introductory remarks by telling the audience that the school's greatest resource is its faculty. He might almost have been reading from the conservatory bulletin, which advertises that:

> The artists and educators who make up the faculty at the Eastern Metropolitan Conservatory are the school's greatest pride. Over the years, the quality and diversity of teachers has been the single most compelling reason for music students to choose the Eastern Metropolitan Conservatory. To study and perform with men and women of such artistic stature forms the heart of a true Conservatory education.

Over 50 percent of the conservatory bulletin (34 of 64 pages) is given to biographical summaries and promotional photographs of the individual faculty members. Thus one source of evidence is in official pronouncements: the primary valuation of faculty artists is a point of official policy at the conservatory.

To make the meaning of such a valuation clear, it should perhaps be mentioned that some other institutions of higher music education do not place the same emphasis on the importance of the faculty members in their public pronouncements, nor has such an emphasis always been present at EMCM. For example, although the quality of its faculty is comparable with that of EMCM, the College of Music at Midland highlights its own modern and extensive rehearsal and performing facilities, and the variety of educational opportunities available on a university campus. Although in this we may be dealing in part with an institution's manner of marketing itself, such representations to the public are certainly not unrelated to the social organizations of the respective institutions. The administrative organization of the Eastern Metropolitan Conservatory is considerably less centralized than that at Midland.

Evidence of the importance of the faculty's artistic merits comes also from the students. When on one occasion I mentioned to a student that fully half of the new conservatory bulletin was devoted to descriptions of the faculty, the prompt response was, "Well, at least they've decided to lead with their strength." Numerous students expressed irritation about what they saw as a highly unsatisfactory institution (from unsatisfying courses and seemingly inappropriate course requirements to run-ins with particular administrative offices) and yet were devoted to or admiring of their own principal teacher. A positive relationship between the student and the individual teacher was felt to be a necessity by almost everyone. Students who encountered serious problems in their relationship with their teacher characteristically tried for a change of teacher or considered changing schools. Other students tended to characterize their dissatisfaction with the conservatory institution as a price to be paid for studying with a high quality private teacher, rather than as a reason for possibly moving to another school.

A different kind of evidence for my point regarding the importance of the teachers' artistic individualism in the educational philosophy of the conservatory came during an interview with a longtime conservatory faculty member and administrator. He told me that on a couple of occasions he had tried unsuccessfully to introduce into the conservatory programs in Orff Schulwerk (a European system of classroom music education for children) and the Suzuki system of violin pedagogy. Both programs had met with considerable resistance from conservatory faculty members. "Why should we have these foreign music education systems in the conservatory?" he paraphrased the reluctant teachers as saying. "Why can't we have our own *conservatory* system?" He laughed quietly and said, "I certainly wouldn't be opposed to a conservatory system, but who's got one?" The fact behind this remark is that the teachers in the conservatory have highly varied and individualized approaches to the teaching of music. The resistance to Orff and Suzuki music pedagogy—as radically contrasting to each other as those two systems are—is over the threat of compelling teachers to follow an approach to music teaching that was worked out elsewhere. The threat is that of reduced individualism.

This same administrator told me that the conservatory avoids the standard academic system of faculty ranking (i.e., as professor, associate professor, and assistant professor) in order to maximize the artistic and to minimize the academic image of the faculty members, hoping to avoid the implication that students studying with a teacher of "Assistant Professor" rank would not be studying with as important a teacher as one ranked as a full "Professor." This explanation is itself probably more significant than the fact of the absence of academic ranking in the conservatory; conservatory students certainly do not perceive all teachers as equivalent simply because none are formally ranked. By far the more important point is that by disregarding the standard system of academic ranking, the conservatory institutionally stresses different criteria of excellence and achievement, namely those associated with the building of an individual reputation as a musician.

Here again, of course, we are dealing in part with a matter of public presentation, at least in the sense that the conservatory students are a consuming "public." However, as another faculty member pointed out, the presence or absence of such formalized academic ranking systems is hardly immaterial in the professional lives of the individual teachers. "That hurts me," he said of the lack of formal academic ranking, "because I'm a classroom teacher rather than a performance teacher, and if I should ever want to get a job in a university it would be very hard to get an appointment at a rank commensurate with my experience. I have no rank here." The professional interests of the classroom teachers—the teachers of music history, music theory, or any of the handful of liberal arts courses offered by the conservatory—are much less reflected in the policy of avoiding the standard professorial ranking than are those of the studio or performance teachers. Indeed, it was the latter group, which of course forms the large majority of the conservatory faculty, that was largely responsible for a vote in the faculty senate favoring the abolition of even the numerical rating system. If adopted by the trustees, this would tend to shift the criteria for such things as setting faculty salaries and teaching assignments, replacing what were relatively impersonal and formal standards with standards that will clearly be more individualistic, artistic, and subjective.

Certainly one of the criteria for evaluating faculty is the number and success of students of the various teachers. The fact that teachers' prestige is augmented by their student's success is mirrored by the fact that students draw status from association with a prestigious teacher, and it is this pattern of reciprocal prestige-lending that grounds my analysis of conservatory social organization in terms of patron-client relationships.

STUDENT: The teacher I have is known as being *so* good, and the fact is, she is. There's like two . . . teachers that are very good here, the rest of them—oh, God, this is on tape!—are not that good. And if I was with anyone else other than those two, first of all the instruction wouldn't be as good, second of all you wouldn't have the . . . certain sense of pride that you're with that teacher and that studio.

HK: What does that mean? You mentioned a sense of pride that you're a Smithson student, which I take it has some meaning in the conservatory ambience, because she's sort of a "star" teacher. Can you say anything specific about what that means for your own music making? When you walk out on stage, does that fact that you're in this at least loosely conceived elite. . . .

STUDENT (*smiling*): Yes, that's true. . . . I want to live up to the kind of reputation that her students have set before me. . . . I remember looking up to the . . . second-year grads, last year, who were her students, and just, you know, thinking "wow!" . . . Being in such awe of them, and thinking that they were so good, and that they were polished, and that they were professional. . . .

And I guess since we care so much for her, too, she believes in us and she takes such personal interest in us that I not only didn't want to let her down, I want to continue the reputation of her students. And we're all close and very supportive of each other as well. . . . If you're in her studio or in Ellen Tatum's, . . . you've got your foot going in the right place, you know, you're lucky, because they are the two best teachers.

Evidence of this kind of organization is to be seen and heard both in and out of the concert halls. "You see those people sitting over there?" a conservatory office worker said to me during lunch, "That's a bunch of self-selected violinists, they're the real top crowd bunch here, really cliquish." Description of conservatory social organization in terms of cliques is certainly valid, and it is a view of many, perhaps most people in the conservatory. However, the internal differentiations of these cliques is frequently recognized in terms of studios, and such differentiations are the locus of much intense negotiating of the musical status of both students and teachers. The word *studio* is frequently used to refer to a group consisting of a teacher and the private students of that teacher. In this way teachers often become nodal persons for student cliques. Clearly, this form of social organization is a fundamental element in the music educational process in the conservatory.

"Being a student here has been very hard for me," said an undergraduate who had transferred into the conservatory from an Ivy League university. "I wouldn't say it's so much a social difficulty," she continued, "as political. I've never experienced politics before, all this cordial chit chat, but people always have their ulterior motive." This student had been unable to make a place for herself in the conservatory woodwind clique and was on that account quite ambivalent regarding her self-image as a musician. She perceived her inability to "crack" the clique as being related in part to her performing skills, or rather, to their lack: "If you're good, then things are okay." There can be little doubt, however, that her inability to make her way into the woodwind clique was tied to the fact that she was very unhappy with her own teacher, who, she feels, is too much concerned with being a nice guy and with political game playing. "He doesn't feel the way I do about music," she said, "and I really hated him for a while." On the other hand, she feels that she is very talented, that "I'm going to make it, I'll be okay," a feeling which is clearly related to her insistence that music and truly musical feelings are pure, safe from political shading. "Music comes from God," she said, "Well, maybe not God, I'm not sure I believe in God, but whatever— energy, the big $E$ . . . and the power that comes from music is a *real* thing. This power over other people, that's fake."

This student was clearly aware of the extent to which the conservatory social environment posed a threat to her own beliefs about music, purity, and power. "I've been ranting and raving about being natural," she said, "but in this environment. . . ." and she just shook her head. The paradox that she articulated might be considered an archetype of conservatory thinking about the social context of music making: the politics of the conservatory are corrupt, but the music remains pure— the grail in a cesspool. The hypocrisy rampant in conservatory cliques spoils things for those with musical integrity or "purity" (though she was talented, things had been very difficult for her, as she couldn't reconcile herself to "playing politics"), and yet on the other hand the sure way to be accepted into such cliques is to be a good musician ("if you're good, you're okay").

These two students represent opposite ends of a continuum in the social organization of the conservatory. Clearly, then, the social organization of conservatory cliques is often closely linked to the personae of the teachers, and student cliques are neither an unmitigated detriment nor an unqualified asset to the process of a musical training in the conservatory. One aspect of cliques is that they are exclusive; this is typically seen as unfortunate and as political. The student who was not accepted into the oboe clique experienced this as a hardship caused by the "political" style of both teacher and students. However, cliques are also solidarity groups, and in this aspect they are experienced as highly beneficial, as exemplified by the comments of the singing student.[3] It should be self-evident that a solidarity group made up of the students of a single teacher necessarily entails some degree of consensus regarding that teacher. Thus the disagreements of the undergraduate oboist with her teacher would have make it all but impossible to be a member of that studio clique.

A student who is highly unsatisfied with her or his teacher may ask to be assigned to a different teacher. The procedure for this is administered within each department, and while such a request is usually granted once requested (my data on this particular point are very limited), the process of making and evaluating such a request puts considerable strain on everyone involved. The musical development of the student, the personal characteristics and teaching style of the present teacher, as well as of the requested teacher, are liable to become specific issues of an official policy decision. All of this, in turn, has considerable impact on the organization of and the dynamics within the studio cliques.

Another manifestation of the link between a teacher and his or her students is the fact that teachers are named on the printed program for student recitals: the performer is named as "student of John Doe." Despite the viewpoint of the voice student already quoted regarding the esteem she felt she accrued from being associated with a particular studio, other students felt that this policy served mainly to transmit esteem from a student performer to the teacher. I will not attempt to assess the relative validity of these two positions beyond saying that it should be clear that the musical esteem of teacher and student are linked by such a policy, and that gains by either almost inevitably accrue also to the other.

The policy of printing the teacher's name on the programs of student performances has a significant counterpart in the pages of the conservatory bulletin. One of the notable features of the lengthy section devoted to faculty sketches in the bulletin is the enumeration of the pedagogical lineages associated with each conservatory teacher.

"Studies with Zara Nelsova, Claus Adam, Leonard Rose, Margaret Rowell, Gregor Piatigorsky," runs the sketch of one of the cello teachers. "Piano with Leonard Shure, Rosina Lhevinne; theory and composition with Martin Boykan, Edward T. Cone, Earl Kim, Roger Sessions," says that of a piano teacher. The names of legendary musicians are sprinkled liberally throughout these pages. Here one sees mentioned the shades of Landowska, Boulanger, Cortot, Szigeti, Thibaud, Flesch, and Steuermann, as well as the still living Serkin, Rampal, Biggs, Copland, Babbitt, and Boulez.

It may appear that I have confused patronage-style organization with lineage organization by presenting pedagogical lineages as evidence of a system of music-education patronage. The point to be made, however, is that the relationships between teachers and students recapitulates the structural principles of political patronage, and that in such a context the pedagogical lineages that are presented in the conservatory bulletin are indications of musical authority, and thus are potential resources for teachers in the recruitment of students. "Study with me," the implicit message runs, "and I will introduce you to the ways of music as transmitted to me by these masters."

Of course, the names listed in these pedagogical lineages are chosen carefully; only the most distinguished names will be mentioned, and not everyone can point to a Schnabel or a Landowska. Thus, some of these genealogies feature names that are at best known only to the most thoroughly initiated. On the other hand, the very presentation of a pedagogical genealogy entails the suggestion that anyone named is or was a distinguished musician, so that to be unacquainted with those named may indicate that it is the reader who is a neophyte rather than the genealogy which is insignificant. Some of the lineages include the names of teachers still at the conservatory.

The importance of all this name dropping, it must be emphasized, is to present each faculty member as the individual conservator of a distinct and distinguished musical heritage. The implicit message is that if one studies with a particular teacher, then one steps into a particular line of musical descent. The most striking example of this comes not from my fieldwork but from my own piano studies in a conservatory graduate program, when at my first lesson with a new teacher, the teacher told me, "my teacher was Artur Schnabel, the famous pianist. Schnabel studied with Theodor Leschetitzky, Leschetitzky studied with Liszt, Liszt studied with Czerny, and of course Czerny was a student of Beethoven. So you see, you come into a good pedigree here."[4] All of this was said in mirth, but certainly not in irony.

From all of this it should be clear that although Western art music is very much a literate cultural idiom, the reproduction and maintenance of this music constitutes an aural tradition. One does not gainsay the importance of the score in saying that even "classical" music does not reside in the printed page. The patterns of social organization of the conservatory must not be dismissed as simply the "political" underbelly of an "artistic" process. To believe otherwise is to retain a commitment to an insidious cultural bias. To be sure, the scholarly appeal to the importance of aural tradition has heretofore been associated primarily with the study of cultural idioms having no system of written notation.[5] Perhaps because of this, it is important to stress that a literate idiom such as "classical" music is also dependent for its meaning, its vitality, and indeed for a major aspect of what it is, on what folklorists, ethnomusicologists, and anthropologists have referred to as aural tradition. The social dynamics of the conservatory are of fundamental importance to the aural tradition of "classical" music.

# The Insurrection: A Case Study in Conservatory Dynamics

In the latter part of the conservatory semester there was what can only be called an insurrection by the members of the conservatory's senior symphony orchestra, which was about to leave for a concert tour in

Europe. Among most people in the conservatory, this insurrection was interpreted mainly in terms of particular personalities, but it also exemplified some important points pertaining to the social organization of the institution. This uprising provides a clear look at the conflict between a centralized authority structure and the relatively decentralized system of patron-client relationships which obtain in the "studio" type of conservatory social organization.

One Friday, about three weeks before the orchestra's departure, the regular orchestra rehearsal ended a few minutes early with the concertmaster making an announcement that everybody clearly knew in advance, namely that two of the school's top administrators had come to discuss the problems of "low morale" in the orchestra. The effect was that of an elementary school teacher's calling in the principal to help enforce discipline: "I don't mean to blame anyone, but I know something's wrong when I hear all this talk about morale problems in the orchestra, and then when today I come to rehearsal I find there's six or eight violins missing, a horn player missing, all these people late to rehearsal," began the administrator. His main theme was "professionalism":

> The bottom line is that . . . we all want to make the best possible music. We can't just give in to the morale problems. It's like old age—not a nice situation, but the alternative is so much worse. We've got to pull together. Rehearse your parts, make the best of it.

When he had finished, a harpist in the orchestra stood up and verbally threw down a gauntlet:

> I can't speak for the rest of the orchestra, but I wasn't very impressed by your pep talk. You tell us all to act like professionals, but I don't feel that I'm treated as though I were expected to

be professional by this school. Yesterday I was supposed to have my recital jury,[6] and of the three faculty members who were supposed to be there, only one showed up, and she was ten minutes late. And the other day, I got into the rehearsal room fifteen minutes early to tune my harp for rehearsal, and when I'm just about finished someone tells me that rehearsal that day is in the concert hall. And this kind of thing happens all the time!

Her rebuke, interrupted once by her own attempt to fight off tears, was received with applause from the players in the orchestra. The administrator acknowledged the validity of her position ("You know what? you're right") but returned immediately to his theme of the importance of professional responsibility on the part of the orchestra players. There followed a welter of complaints from the students about issues ranging from poor communications regarding rehearsals to the fact that many of them simply felt that the orchestra was playing poorly. However, apart from some matters concerning the schedule of the tour, these issues were not discussed in any detail. The closest thing to an answer to such complaints was a brief speech by the administrator in praise of the conductor, Tom Vosniak.

Indeed, for most students Vosniak was the entire issue in the matter, and one student commented to me later that the harpist should not have raised the issues of her recital jury "because we've got enough problems just in the orchestra." I was first made aware of the intensity of the strife among the orchestra players by the student who pointed out to me that at one point someone had put a note on the orchestra bulletin board urging players to refuse to show up at a special rehearsal called by Vosniak. I several times noticed what I perceived to be an unusual amount of talking among orchestra players during rehearsal, and when I asked students about this, my suspicions were energetically confirmed. "Oh, yes, it's gotten to be really belligerent," as one cellist put it. What was happening, in effect, was the equivalent of what in a factory would be a work stoppage.

Significantly, the issue of professionalism, which was used by the administrator in his efforts to restore discipline to the orchestra, was also used in the complaints by the students against the conductor. Students repeatedly contrasted the conservatory orchestra, peopled with players who are at the beginning of a musical profession, with a local amateur orchestra conducted by Vosniak, suggesting that the current difficulties were the result of Vosniak's trying to do in the conservatory orchestra the same things he does with his amateur orchestra. "The stuff that's going on over in the Community Symphony [the amateur orchestra], that's really gross," said a violinist in the conservatory orchestra. He said that the Community Symphony is just made up of people who are "trying to get in good with Vosniak," and while he clearly felt the conservatory orchestra provided some contrast with this, he also felt that an important part of the problem in the conservatory orchestra came from Vosniak's attempts to replicate the dynamic of the Community Symphony. He said that Vosniak calls students on the phone, asking their opinions on interpretation of the orchestra's repertoire, something that he characterized as "recruiting" conservatory students as supporters for his own conducting.

There was intense and widespread resentment among students of Vosniak's predilection for playing favorites, of his political manipulations of the players in the orchestra. Several complaints focused on arbitrary changes of the players' seating.[7] One complaint dealt with a student who was urged by Vosniak to join the orchestra with promises of several prominent parts to play, but at a rehearsal for the piece in question, the student found a note on his chair saying that someone else was to sit first chair for this piece, and thus that he would not be playing the part he had in effect been promised. "This is all political," one student explained to me, "but you can't prove it, because there are musical judgments going on at the same time."

Another complaint that I heard repeatedly was that the orchestra frequently played badly out of tune, and that Vosniak did nothing to correct the orchestra's sloppy intonation. This was indeed one of the complaints raised during the meeting with the conservatory administrators at the end of rehearsal. In a rehearsal a couple of weeks after that meeting, Vosniak, perhaps trying to meet that very criticism, stopped the orchestra to tell the tympanist that he was playing out of tune. The importance, the subtlety, and the complexity of this problem—as well as the erosion of authority in the conductor's role—became apparent with the tympanist's reply. "I'm not playing out of tune," he said. "I'm in tune; the orchestra's out of tune." Apart from shattering the stereotype of the orchestra conductor as authoritarian martinet, his reply quickly brought the exchange into areas seemingly several times removed from the problem. "Why don't you all tune more carefully?" said Vosniak to the rest of the orchestra. For answer, members of the brass section complained that they couldn't tune because the seats for the brass were not in place when the orchestra was tuning, since the stage manager hadn't been told that the orchestra would be rehearsing this particular repertoire today.[8]

Although it is surely safe to assume that no conservatory student would say that what they wanted from a conductor was an authoritative martinet, there certainly were complaints that Vosniak was indecisive and insecure as a conductor. "He just doesn't know what he wants to do sometimes," said one student. "He'll stop and ask the orchestra how he should conduct something, and when one section says to do it one way and another section says to do it another, he just has to apologize for changing back and forth. It's bad, because it shows the orchestra that you're not in command."

Even his strongest detractors, however, would not deny that Vosniak is an intensely musical man, and many of the most adverse comments were followed with remarks on the order of "but he's really musical, got a lot of good ideas." The problem was that Vosniak's strengths as a musician were incompatible with the role expectations of an orchestral conductor. "All Vosniak cares about is if you play musically, get the expression. He doesn't care anything about intonation or ensemble," said one student. Despite the variety of issues raised in this episode, this one seems to me to be the keystone to an understanding of the dissension in the conservatory orchestra. It was some of the very traits that had for years made Vosniak highly successful in the conservatory as a conducting teacher and chamber music instructor that led to the unrest in the conservatory orchestra.

The value of playing (or singing) "musically" is a genuinely sacred value in the conservatory, quite possibly the ultimate value, and Vosniak's enthusiasm in eliciting "musical" performances from his students has apparently been a hallmark of his teaching for as long as he has been at the conservatory. It is clear that he has consistently had a collection of enthusiastic followers among the conservatory students, one that diminished because of the dissension in the orchestra, but also one that will surely be restored when Vosniak returns to teaching chamber music classes full-time.

In one of my earliest interviews at the conservatory, a graduate piano student told me that her study with Vosniak had been the most valuable association she had had in this institution. Significantly, she told me that when she was still a new student in the conservatory Vosniak called her on the phone to congratulate her on how well she had played in his class that day. Obviously, his enthusiasm for her musicality was an important basic element in her feelings about his value as a teacher, and Vosniak's practise of calling on the phone to discuss musical values with particular students he admired was clearly not limited to his dealings with the orchestra. In the context of his smaller chamber music classes, this enthusiastic interaction with individual students could be seen as little more than a normal extension of his quest for intensely "musical" playing. In the context of the orchestra, however, it inevitably came to be seen as unfair favoritism and manipulation.

By the end of my stay at the conservatory, this same piano student—who was not a member of the orchestra, but who like everyone else had heard all the gossip about the difficulties in the orchestra—had herself come to distrust Vosniak, saying that she wouldn't ever be able to recommend him to another student. "He thinks he's serving the music," she said, "he thinks that if a student is musical, then the best way to get a good performance is to recruit and support that student and to treat those support relationships as obligations." Given this student's high opinion of her own musicality (something that came out very clearly in the earlier interview), this statement could very well have been incorporated into her earlier enthusiasm for Vosniak were it not for the last phrase, "and to treat those support relationships as obligations." This too shows the inextricability of the link between "musical" and "political" concerns within the conservatory.

The preceding discussion can be seen as a supplement to Robert Faulkner's discussion of authority relationships in a symphony orchestra. The members of the conservatory orchestra would certainly confirm Faulkner's statement that "a conductor must create respect for himself. He is not accorded a fixed distribution of deference because of the position he occupies" (Faulkner 1973: 149). Moreover, the dissension in the conservatory orchestra is a striking example of his comment that the lack of perceived authority in the conductor can result in "subsequent conduct such as open disrespect, sullenness, deliberately lowered work effort, selective inattention, sarcasm, and in general the making and taking of role distance" (1973: 151).

Faulkner's discussion, however, deals with a professional orchestra, and specifically with the attitudes of orchestra players toward short-term guest conductors. In such a context, "musicians agree that it takes about ten or fifteen minutes for an orchestra faced with a new maestro to determine whether he is a fake, a phony, a brilliant technician, a charismatic personality, or a poseur" (1973: 149). While Faulkner claims that "similar standards are applied to permanent conductors" (1973: 149), it seems unlikely that the same haste in evaluation would obtain in the case of a permanent conductor, who would have a very different place in the overall authority structure of the orchestra, including, for example, a formalized and perhaps personal relationship with the orchestra's board of directors.

Tom Vosniak was neither a short-term visiting conductor nor the permanent conductor of the conservatory orchestra. He held a one-year appointment, and during the period of my research a search and screen process was under way to select a permanent conductor. Unlike the conductors discussed by Faulkner's informants, however, Vosniak was unquestionably *the* conductor of the orchestra during the period of research.

The analytic significance of the dissension in the conservatory orchestra does not lie in the dynamics of authority in the preparation of particular performances, as was the case in Faulkner's study. Rather, it lies in the perspective it affords an examination of the organization of authority in the broader institution of the conservatory. Over and above being a performing organization, the orchestra is an institutional structure that constitutes a nexus of a wide variety of musical and organizational problems in the conservatory. Despite one student's complaint that the harpist should not have interjected nonorchestral issues into the discussion of professionalism and orchestra morale, the orchestra is, as one of the administrators acknowledged, a structured repository of administrative problems affecting the conservatory as an institution.

It would be a mistake, therefore, to confine an analysis of the dissension in the conservatory orchestra solely to an assessment of Tom Vosniak's musical personality, or to his inability to communicate authority from the podium. While Faulkner's study presented authority in the orchestra as a function of the conductor's personal presence and his skill in rehearsing the orchestra, a crucial fact of the present case is that sources of authority in the conservatory orchestra are by no means confined to situations of orchestral performances and rehearsals. The postrehearsal session with the two senior conservatory administrators provides a superficial example of this point, and there are more pervasive, although less self-evident, illustrations of this as well.

Although I did not systematically gather data on this point, the fact that Vosniak had been given only a one-year appointment as conductor of the orchestra was surely a significant element in the authority structure of the orchestra. While it would be farfetched to suggest that the problems of discipline in the orchestra would have been remedied by changing Vosniak's contract from a one-year term to a permanent appointment, it is certainly not insignificant to call attention to the willingness in the conservatory to put such a "lame duck" conductor in this position. Numerous students and faculty mentioned to me the likelihood that the next year's conductor would again be a single-year appointee. While their explanations for this consistently referred to notions such as the necessity of a "trial period" and the importance of making sure that the right person was eventually selected, the widespread willingness to tolerate a transient state of affairs in the conservatory orchestra calls for additional explanation.

There can be no doubt that among many instrumentalist teachers and students in the conservatory—perhaps particularly among string players, who make up the bulk of the orchestra—there is an effective "anti-orchestra" sentiment. Although the symphony orchestra is a prominent element in the conservatory's public image—the tour in Europe provides a striking example of this—involvement in and commitment to orchestra playing is perceived by many as a threat to the students' commitment to their individual musical and professional development. Time spent in learning orchestral parts is time that might be spent developing one's own artistic skills on the instrument, and it is the latter that is quite generally perceived as the primary agenda for a conservatory student.

In another study, Faulkner (1971: 52–68) points out a difference between string players and wind players in the Hollywood studio orchestras regarding their youthful career expectations. Brass and woodwind players tended to have selected orchestra playing as a career by the age of twenty, an age at which many violinists and cellists still held aspirations for solo careers. Although Faulkner does not attempt to explain this differential, there is a factor involved here which is surely an element also in the "anti-orchestra" sentiment in the conservatory, at least among the string players. The literature of "classical" music contains many masterworks written for individual string players, and there is a strong tendency for violinists and cellists to conceive of artistic development in terms of, say, playing the great sonatas of Beethoven rather than playing the violin parts in the Beethoven symphonies. There is, however, much less solo literature for most wind instruments. A trumpeter is almost necessarily more inclined to conceive of musical development in terms of the most prominent and most difficult trumpet passages in the standard orchestral literature.[9]

The following comments were made by a violinist in the conservatory orchestra, perhaps mainly about other string players:

> STUDENT: A lot of kids up there only play in orchestra because they want to have lessons.... They just sort of switch off; they don't consider that music.
>
> HK: What?
>
> STUDENT: You have to play in the orchestra to be in school.
>
> HK: So that's—
>
> STUDENT: So they don't even think about that as being music, it's just—*orchestra*.

While I never heard an orchestra member state that he or she harbored such sentiments while playing in the orchestra, numerous students concluded their explanation of "the Vosniak problem" in the orchestra with remarks to the effect that playing in the orchestra was viewed by many as an unpaid service performed by students for the benefit of the conservatory. The expression "anti-orchestra" was given to me by a conservatory theory teacher, who used the phrase to refer collectively to the applied study faculty (the teachers of the various instruments). He claimed that it was the opinion of the applied study faculty that students should be practising eight hours a day and preparing for careers as recitalists rather than working in orchestras. This teacher was certainly not alone in this view—it was also articulated to me by various students and may well have been held by other faculty members—but I cannot accept it at face value as an explanation of the dissension in the conservatory orchestra.

When I challenged the theory teacher by asking if the applied faculty really felt their students could make careers as concert virtuosi, his answer was of an aren't-they-being-absurd nature. Nevertheless, the economic realities that confront the graduate of a music conservatory in the 1980s are surely lost on nobody, not even the applied study (performance) faculty. Although explicit and implicit admonitions abound to the effect that the only route to a musical career is that of disciplined and arduous practising, this should not be taken as proof that the primary concern of the applied study faculty is to assure their disciples of successful careers, desirable though that may be.

The orientation favoring individual development of artistic technique and repertoire by conservatory students should not be taken solely as indicating a "damn the torpedoes" attitude toward unpleasant economic realities among either faculty or students. While actors' perceptions of future situations are of course a crucial element in the understanding of present social developments, the concrete exigencies of the present are surely as important to social action as more abstract projections of the future.

Although it is only occasionally spoken aloud, there is a general understanding that only a small minority of the graduates of the conservatory will be able to make professional careers as performing musicians. "If the conservatory only admitted students who could make a career in music, we'd have to close our doors tomorrow" was the way the placement counselor put it. Clearly, the ongoing practise of the teachers and administrators of the conservatory is not oriented simply toward preparing young musicians for a professional career.

The orientation of conservatory practise pertains more directly to the maintenance of the institution of the conservatory itself. The stress placed in the conservatory on developing solo repertoire and technique is intertwined with the reproduction of the institution of the conservatory, particularly of the social organization focused on what I have described as studio cliques. The "anti-orchestra" sentiments are in part a function of a social organization in which individual studios form corporate groups. The notion that extensive commitment to orchestral work is likely to hinder a student's musical development cannot meaningfully be said to benefit the student's future professional career. In many cases, however, it can be seen to contribute to a studio-centered social organization in the conservatory. What is generally articulated as a "musical" concern (this kind of musical development is more valuable than that kind of musical development) is thus at least in part a social organizational concern. A student's commitment to solo technique is in effect a commitment to a relationship with an individual mentor.

Conservatory students characteristically speak in praise of the high quality of the faculty while grousing about the confusion that emanates from administrative offices and the disquiet in the orchestra. However, this division of perceptions into contrasting "strengths" and "weaknesses" tends to conceal the fact that these factors are elements of a single organizational structure. A powerful centralized structure of authority—whether in a dean's office or on the orchestra podium—would tend to undermine the strength of the "studio" social organization in the conservatory, the primacy of the artistic individuality of the faculty members, and in turn the aural tradition of musical performance that these faculty members serve to maintain.

# THREE

# CREAM RISES

## A Musical Context

Conservatory life is about talent. Musical talent is at once the most pervasive phenomenon and the biggest issue in conservatory life. While everyone in the conservatory "has" talent (that is, everyone feels that she or he is talented and is perceived by certain others, such as various teachers and admissions committees, as having talent), it is also the case that nearly all of them, or at least nearly all students, are very much concerned with how much talent they have, and sometimes with whether they "really" have talent at all. On the other hand, while conservatory life is unquestionably about talent, it cannot be said that talent, even musical talent, is associated uniquely or even primarily with conservatories and music schools. Thus, in an important sense the cultural dynamics of "talent" constitute an important context of music making in the conservatory. An examination of talent, then, provides a context for music making in the conservatory perhaps more significant, for example, than a description of the urban neighborhood in which the conservatory sits, a tabulation of the ethnic groups or income brackets represented in the faculty and student body, or the types of funding that support the institution.

Two facets of the "context" notion should be briefly distinguished. First, a *context* is an environment that lends meaning or significance to something. Second, whenever X is a context for Y, then Y can also be seen to be a context for X. To say that the dynamics of talent constitute a context of conservatory music making entails the corresponding fact that music making is a significant context for understanding talent. Once again, "contexts" are not independent of autonomous domains, but rather are reciprocal and interdependent. At issue, then, are not just particular contexts, but rather a dynamic of contextualization, what one might call a cultural intercontextuality.[1]

# A Cultural Representation

The notion of "talent" is, of course, germane to many musical idioms, and perhaps even more to various nonmusical arenas. While I suspect that in some social circles there is still a belief that little talent is required or expected in pop or rock music, such a belief seems to have much less circulation than when I was a child taking my first piano lessons. One factor in this development is surely the advent, over the last two decades, of a rhetoric of criticism for "popular" music (until the mid 1960s, journalist music criticism pertained only to what is generally called "classical" or "serious" music) and even more recently, the inclusion of "popular" music in some formal educational curricula. The idea that rock music required little or no talent seems to have been associated with the idea that it needed no teaching. In recalling conversations with my former Midland colleagues regarding whether or not music could truly be taught, it has more than once occurred to me that the dynamics of talent entail the irony that in music education, it is the talented few who can be taught that which may in the end be unteachable.

The notion of "talent" is so fundamental to Western thinking about human musicality that it perhaps still needs to be emphasized that differentials in musical or esthetic talent are not to be found everywhere. Various anthropologists have noted the lack of such a concept where social and esthetic values are markedly different from those of Western society, along with a corresponding lack of significant differentiation of musical ability among the people. Perhaps the best-known example of this comes from John Blacking's *How Musical is Man?*, an essay on musicality among the Venda of South Africa. Blacking points out that Western notions of musical talent "are diametrically opposed to the Venda idea that all normal human beings are capable of musical performance" (Blacking 1973: 34), and that among the Venda, musical "accuracy is always expected and sentiment generally assumed" (1983: 37).

Moreover, the Venda are anything but unique. In *The Ethonomusicology of the Flathead Indians* (1967), Alan P. Merriam quotes one of his informants on the matter of criteria for evaluating singers as follows:

A man is a good singer because he has a good voice and because his lungs and voice are good and strong. X has a good memory for songs. He remembers the War Dance, the Owl Dance, the Gift Dance songs.

APM: If I had good lungs and throat would I be a good singer? I am big and strong; does this mean I would be a good singer if I knew the songs and could remember them?

Yes, you would be a good singer.

APM: Anybody can be a good singer?

Yes, if his lungs and throat are strong, and he can remember the songs, he would be a good singer. (Merriam 1967: 50)

Similarly, Christopher Marshall reports (1982: 169) that among the Debarcani, a Macedonian peasant group in southwestern Yugoslavia, "musical talent is . . . thought to be distributed equally to all." Steven Feld, discussing Western notions of special communicative competences such as musical "talent," states that "nothing parallel exists among the Kaluli" of Papua New Guinea (Feld 1984: 390). Perhaps the most forceful statement on this issue is John Messenger's account of the Anang Ibibio of Nigeria:

We were constantly amazed at the musical abilities displayed by these people, especially by the children who, before the age of five, can sing hundreds of songs both individually and in choral groups and, in addition, are able to play several percussion instruments and have learned dozens of intricate dance movements calling for incredible muscular control. We searched in vain for the "non-musical" person, finding it difficult to make inquiries about tone deafness and its assumed effects because the Anang language possesses no comparable concept.... They will not admit, as we tried so hard to get them to, that there are those who lack the requisite abilities. This same attitude applies to the other esthetic areas. Some dancers, singers and weavers are considered more skilled than most, but everyone can dance and sing well. (Messenger 1958: 20–22)

Nevertheless, the fact that some people can't, as some would say, "carry a tune in a bucket" is for many people an unexamined given of everyday social experience, rather than being viewed as a particular characteristic of Western society. Indeed, the preceding quotations from Merriam and Messenger indicate how difficult it can be even for professional anthropologists to fully accept non-Western notions regarding talent and musicality. The analysis of musical "talent" in this chapter will proceed along lines similar to those taken in anthropological analyses of extraordinary powers that accrue to special persons, powers such as religious charisma, spirit possession, or witchcraft. That is to say, the present analysis treats musical talent as a cultural representation. Such a treatment is in radical opposition to the position of Lévi-Strauss (1969: 18), who contends that the distinction between those who "secrete" music and those who do not is so profound, so obvious, and yet so mysterious that musicians are in effect like gods!

Not the least important aspect of an analysis of talent is the fact that it brings us directly to a discussion of inequalities of social esteem, authority, and power, something that is a basic element in any social process. One of the most basic aspects of the notion of talent is that of differentiation: some people have tremendous amounts of talent; some have little or none; many have talent in some areas but not in others. Talent thus conceived is understood as located "in" the person's mind, psyche, or perceptual apparatus, and is widely felt to be transmitted genetically, like hair and eye color. Talent, then, is a representation of differentials of potential for certain socially valued behavior, differentials that are believed to be ordained not in social order but rather by the inherent nature of people.

The concept of "potential," however, is generally cumbersome and unavailing in analyses of social behavior, and a starting point in this study is the idea that musical behavior is a particular kind of social behavior. The validity of a notion of "potential" entails an understanding of the process through which the potential will be realized or activated. For example, the concept of potential energy is premised on the understanding that specific physical and mechanical processes can generate kinetic energy from the store of potential. Although there are, to be sure, biological and physiological mechanisms of the body that are affected by musical behavior, attempts at analytic isolation of musical potential by psychologists and neurologists have consistently been very problematic. The idea of musical "potential" is wedded to an implicit idea that musical experience is not so much social as intrapersonal. The study of human musicality—whether it be under the rubric of musical "aptitude," musical "intelligence," or talent—will surely be riddled with difficulties as long as the focus is on the individual rather than on social interaction.

Nevertheless, "talent" is widely understood as a form of potential, as is illustrated by the fact that it is frequently contrasted conceptually with an actual skill. Indeed, it is widely believed that one might well have a considerable amount of talent and yet not be an accomplished musician, due to lack of training. I confronted a striking example of this during my tenure as a conservatory administrator, when once I was asked to audition a college freshman. He had just graduated as valedictorian of his high-school class and won a college scholarship on the merits of his extremely high grades, especially in natural sciences. However, during the summer before starting college he had begun piano lessons and had made a considerable impression on family and friends with his rapid development, so much so that he had begun to have fairly intense hopes of becoming a concert artist. He discussed his aspirations with an admissions officer, who asked me to listen to him play, not to determine whether or not he could be admitted to the conservatory right away (it was acknowledged in advance that his technical proficiency was not up to conservatory standards), but to determine if his playing gave evidence of a certain something which presaged a future Serkin, Richter, or Rubinstein. It was with some reluctance that I agreed to listen to him play, and the role in which I found myself that day forced me to deal with an aspect of talent which is often overlooked. In that I was explicitly asked to listen not just to his playing but also for an inaudible inner personal trait, I was in effect being asked not just for musical evaluation but for divination.

Within a conservatory, however, the concern is usually focused less on the talent of untrained beginners than on the talent or "musicality" of students who have been through considerable training. Even here, however, things are rarely simple or clear-cut, for while talent is taken as a *terra firma* reality for all conservatory musicians, something which, supposedly, either you have or you don't, nevertheless, musicians frequently disagree regarding who is and who isn't talented. What is more, even sophisticated musicians occasionally reverse themselves regarding a particular individual's musicality or talent.

# The Flunked Promotional

One Thursday toward the end of my stay at EMCM, I was greeted by one of my friends with the exclamation, "Everything's changed!" This was from Johanna, a student whom I had gotten to know through attending the "diction for singers" class, and her news was that although she had been planning to spend the week trying to find herself a summer job, she had been altogether too upset to do any job-hunting because on Monday she had been given failing grades in her year-end promotional audition by the members of the voice faculty. While promotional auditions are routine in the sense that everyone has to have one, flunking the promotional immediately places a student's future at the conservatory in serious doubt. The promotional audition deals with only one aspect of a student's work, but the aspect it deals with is utterly paramount: in the conservatory, failure in musical performance is failure—period. In Johanna's case, for example, her failing grades had been accompanied by suggestions from the voice faculty regarding other fields she should consider studying instead of music.

The gravity of Johanna's failing her promotional was grounded in the fact that although the voice faculty agreed that she had a wonderful singing voice, they had found her to be very "unmusical." This is a serious judgment, for it is commonly held among conservatory musicians—and it was explicitly stated by several of the voice teachers—that a person either is or isn't "musical," and on such a matter there is little that can be done to change things one way or the other. The statements that Johanna was "unmusical" were parallel in their thrust with saying that she was untalented. The voice faculty's judgment of Johanna was in effect a statement of doom; drawing musical expression from an untalented or an unmusical person is taken, in the conservatory, to be about as easy as squeezing blood from a stone.

However, Johanna's distress was complicated by the fact that at the previous year's promotional she had been characterized by several of these same voice teachers as very "musical" indeed; apparently the passage of time and the rush of myriad auditions had obliterated their memory of her previous promotional. Because of both my research interests and my earlier experience in counseling conservatory students, I spent many hours during the next few days discussing with Johanna the implications of her promotional grades. Throughout this period she expended a tremendous amount of emotional and mental energy trying to establish what the word *musical* meant, as well as the word *unmusical*. In a very real sense, she was both: these contradictory reports from the singing teachers had in effect become a part of her person. She was extremely confused.

Johanna was struggling to maintain a self-definition in the face of conflicting characterizations of her by people in power over her. "Nobody can tell me how good I am," she said at one point, "I know how good I am." Nevertheless, people *had* told her how good she was, and she had been very much affected by the experience, and now had considerable doubt about just how good she was. Occasionally she rejected the judgments that she was unmusical: "They say I've got a good instrument [voice], and that I'm a really good actor, and if you have a great voice, and are a good actor, then you have to be somewhat musical, don't you?" On the other hand, while she may not have completely believed or accepted the reports, she had nevertheless "internalized" them. The negative assessments were too weighty to be quickly dismissed. Although she was willing, indeed eager, to discuss with me her feelings about the promotional, she could not bring herself to show me the written reports from the voice teachers. She said that she felt tempted to show them to me, but that she was not sure I would still trust that she was a good singer (she knew that I had never heard her sing).

Johanna readily acknowledged that her performance in the promotional audition had been lackluster. She several times said that the comments on the faculty's audition reports were "accurate," that the faculty had not said anything about her singing that was untrue. She repeatedly said that her singing at the audition had been "detached," that although she had been looking forward to the performance, a few minutes before it she had become very nervous and anxious, and thus her singing had been detached. She said she knew that she had not done well, but also that she would not have believed she could have flunked.

As it happened, Johanna was in due time able to reinstate herself in the conservatory's voice department. When the contradiction between the reports from the earlier and the more recent promotional audition was brought to the attention of the department chairman, the more recent performance was, in effect, re-evaluated, and the next year Johanna resumed study in the conservatory, although now with a different teacher. Two years later, she had performed her recital and completed her degree. The last time I saw her, she was a waitress in a restaurant not far from the conservatory.

# The Cultural Dynamics of Talent

Johanna's promotional raises a set of questions regarding the relation between reality and the way we know reality. Moreover, the events surrounding her promotional involve principles of talent that are also found in countless other environments both inside and outside the conservatory.

To begin with, the dynamics of talent entail an element of temporality; an appraisal of talent is, in effect, an *ex post facto* judgment. If you bring your daughter to a music teacher for an appraisal of her musicality or talent, such an appraisal can and will be made only after she has played or sung. The idea is that talent is "in" a person before, or rather, whether or not, any auditions or performances have taken place. As the members of the voice faculty told Johanna, you either have it or you don't, and there really isn't anything to be done to change things. There is, however, something that can be done to determine these things: the presence or absence of musicality or talent is established on the basis of some sort of performance or audition.

Thus, although "talent" is understood as a form of potential existing independently from performance, attributions of talent, musicality, or their absence come as judgments of actual auditions or performances.[2]

From this it follows that one person's talent is attributed to him or her by someone else, and that the person making the attribution becomes an important element of the first person's very talent. The principle involved is this: if Jack is acknowledged to be a musical ignoramus, then the talent that he attributes to Jill is likely to have almost no validity at all. On the other hand, if Jack is, say, a local school music teacher, then Jill's musical talent is likely to take on at least some importance. Similarly, if after Jack has attributed talent to Jill, a renowned professor from the music conservatory makes a negative assessment of her talent, then our sense of her talent will have been further delimited. The point is that our perception of Jill's talent is not derived simply from an understanding of Jill *qua* Jill. Rather, it derives from our understanding of the relationship between Jack and the conservatory professor and of their respective positions in the community. The validity of a given person's musical talent is a direct function of the relative esteem of the persons who have attributed the talent to the person in question.[3]

The case of Johanna's promotional exposes yet another aspect of this cultural process. Johanna's promotional shows not only that one cannot understand her musicality and talent in terms of Johanna *qua* Johanna, but also that one is not dealing with something that can be understood as talent *qua* talent or as musicality *qua* musicality, a thing-in-itself with a reality independent of the way in which it is determined. The intensity of Johanna's confusion lay in the fact that it was impossible for her to dismiss the negative evaluations from her detractors in the voice department without calling into question what she, for at least the past year, had taken herself to be: a "musical" person.

For a meaningful assessment of musical talent to take place, some listener must, at least implicitly, be able to claim a certain amount of critical knowledge and authority. The basis of such a claim is highly variable; both within and outside a conservatory, highly trained singers, for example, may hesitate to comment on the merits of pianists. The fact that many people decline to make any such verbal evaluative commentary is obvious, but deserves this remark: people who claim to know nothing about music are in effect defining themselves as persons who do not or will not make evaluative critical commentary on musical performances. The meaning of such familiar remarks as "I really don't know much about that kind of music" or "I'm just a singer, I don't know much about piano" is not to be found on the propositional surface of the statement. The import of such a statement is to present the speaker in a recognizable role, namely that of noncritic or outsider.

There is likely to be an important reason for this. Such people may think that if they were to make critical commentary in terms of their own knowledge of music they would be perceived by others as embarrassingly ignorant and might be liable to some form of ridicule. It should be appreciated that presenting oneself as an uncritical listener is frequently an adaptive response to some form of previous embarrassment. Previous social encounters may have established the person's self-image with regard to musical commentary such that taking the role of commentator or critic is perceived as inappropriate or risky.

In light of this, it will be instructive to view critical evaluative commentary on music as verbal performance. For example, among many people, a question such as "What did you think of the Beethoven?" has effectively become conventionalized as the lead-in to a performance of critical sophistication. As such, the question bears a structural similarity with expressions such as "did you hear the one about . . .," or "once upon a time," since both expressions frame a particularly charged contextualization of talk. The perspicacity of a given person's critical commentary is very much at issue, since the critical commentary is itself subject to evaluation and judgment.

Verbal performance is also an emergent quality (Bauman 1977: 37–45) of commentary on music in day-to-day life. A question such as "what did you think of Jill's Beethoven?" very often incurs an emotional dilemma of how to respond (is this person trying to "one-up" me?). As already suggested, some people will respond with some variant of "well, I really don't know anything about that kind of music," thus keeping the intensity of the performance context quite low. Others may be quite willing to perform in the role of critic, in which case there may follow a real matching of musical wits. In the case of Johanna's promotional, of course, the critical evaluations came in the context of the structure of the conservatory institution, and the verbal commentary took the form of formal written reports.

The self-consciousness of an instrumentalist or singer is undoubtedly even more significant. In this context, a useful comparison might be made between the music student who puts in hours preparing for a performance and the teenager who rehearses smoking a cigarette in front of a mirror (Goffman 1974: 63; cf. also Geertz 1973: 5–10). Such a juxtaposition may seem incongruous if not vulgar, and yet the similarities can be instructive. In each case we have an instance of a person self-consciously preparing a performance which will have bearing on her or his social esteem or status. The point of importance here is the extent to which practising the piano does indeed constitute preparation for the musical negotiation of social esteem.

With regard to the analysis of "talent" or "musicality," then, the question is, on what basis will a critic make his judgment? Johanna's critics commented that she frowned a lot during her audition, and complained that she seemed not to like singing; she herself said that her singing had been "detached." Somewhat more generally, a person whose playing is said to sound "mechanical," or "contrived," or for instrumentalists "like a finger drill," will to that extent be considered unmusical or not talented. A person whose performance is "expressive" or "from the heart" and "with feeling" will conversely be considered to be talented. A person will be judged "musical," as distinguished from "accomplished," to the extent that the performance was not, or could not have been, determined by self-conscious preparation, such as systematic rehearsing, formal lessons, and technical drills. An anthropological understanding of musical talent hinges on an appreciation of emotional "feeling" and the tension between self-consciousness and other-consciousness in a musical performance situation.

Rehearsing, whether for the musician or for the teenage smoker, thus entails the paradox of contriving to appear natural. In both cases social acceptance will be contingent upon successfully concealing the contrived (read, self-conscious), and manifesting the "natural" (read, other-conscious), properties of behavior. Ultimately, of course, this ties musical performance and criticism to issues of sincerity and hypocrisy. It is intuitively self-evident that a person "should" always behave sincerely and never "deceptively," and yet such categories are very ambiguous, sometimes nearly inverted, in the context of music criticism. The concealment of artifice is a basic tenet in much Western music and art criticism, and the gamut of ethical and moral values in music criticism is not congruent with that pertaining to a teenager's rehearsed smoking. This complicates but should not obscure the fact that there is an ethical or moral basis to the values manifested in musical evaluation.

An authoritatively stated attribution of "talent" retroactively transforms a succession of social events into the manifestation of intrapersonal traits of an individual. Geertz's phrase, "the immobilization of time through the iteration of form" (1973: 374) is appropriate here, although in this case what we have is a symbolic reversal of time in the constitution of the person. An authoritative assessment of "talent" has the effect, after the fact, of what Austin (1962: 6) called a performative utterance. Such an evaluation constitutes an important element in the individual's personal nature. When a respected musician says "Mrs. Jones, your child is very talented," his evaluation becomes an element of the parent's very love for the child, and indeed of everyone's perception of who the child is, has been, and may be.

The retroactive dynamic of the performative utterance was very much in evidence both before and after Johanna's promotional. A year earlier, the voice faculty had said that she was very musical and talented. It must be recognized that this earlier evaluation was an important factor in Johanna's saying, a year later, when the evaluations were so strikingly reversed, "They can't tell me how good I am, I know how good I am." Indeed, she may well have known how good she was, but an important way she knew was by having been told so by the conservatory voice faculty. And in spite of her brave rejoinder, she at bottom had been made unsure of how good she was: after all, some very authoritative people had just said she was unmusical.

Johanna's promotional illustrates the fact that the "environment" of a person's musical development must be understood in terms of personal relationships characterized by some degree of intimacy and vulnerability. The environment in which a person's musicality is developed is that of intimate personal relationships as they bear on musical experience, including here the emotional vulnerability of the person whose musical development is in question. The nature-nurture question with regard to talent and musicality is poorly dealt with when the "nurture" side of the issue is conceived in terms of such issues as the presence or absence of stereo equipment or musical instruments in the home, or the performance skills and musical tastes of the parents.

In general, after an authoritative "Jack" (or "Wolfgang," or "Vladimir") has made the judgment that "Jill" is not talented, it will probably become inappropriate for Jill to play or sing in Jack's presence: her music will in all probability be perceived as something of a nuisance to him, and listening to her a waste of his good time. Moreover, if Jack's musical opinions are widely influential or if his opinion is widely shared, the social appropriateness of her music making will become problematic in many if not all social situations. The performance of music before any audience can be frightening, but performing before an audience that is disapproving in advance results in almost certain ostracism. Audience response will run along lines of "Doesn't she realize how bad she sounds?"

An authoritative negative judgment tends to become a proscription against subsequent musical-social behavior.[4] Conversely, a judgment that a young child is talented is likely to have the effect of providing her or him with a music-nurturing environment. Not only will such children get plenty of opportunities to perform, but they will be given lessons, encouragement, and various types of special attention and affection. The domain of music, in which attributions of talent are balanced by injunctions against those judged to be unmusical, contrasts significantly with the domain of speech and language acquisition. Prohibitive deprecations of communicative action are generally not found in connection with language learning.

For example, I have a young friend who as a five-year-old was unable to master the pronunciation of such words as "shirt," "birth," and "hurt." For a considerable period she said "short," "borth," and "hort." For much, if not all, of that time she was quite aware that her pronunciations were wrong by adult standards (she would giggle playfully when she heard somebody imitate her pronunciation), but she was never given to understand that her pronunciations were inappropriate for her: she was never told that she should stop saying those words. Childhood performances of language skills may be viewed as idiosyncratic, as "baby talk," or as just plain wrong, but the cultural expectations are that every healthy child will learn to speak normally. Infantile aberrations are understood to be transitory and essentially insignificant. By contrast, childhood performances of music are typically evaluated very carefully for indications of talent, and the possibilities for subsequently learning musical performance skills are very much contingent upon adult evaluations.

The principle of enjoining music making by persons judged to be "untalented" or "unmusical" can be seen in an intensified form in the context of Johanna's promotional. The negative evaluation (that Johanna was "unmusical") from the voice faculty was accompanied by their suggestions of other fields in which she might study, with the clear implication that she might not be allowed to stay at the conservatory. And just as Johanna herself had said that her singing in the promotional audition had been "detached," she also indicated that her relationship with her teacher of the past two years had itself been rather detached and personally unsatisfactory. Johanna's experience made a striking contrast with that of the singing student quoted in the previous chapter, who in her singing took such encouragement from the strong relationship she had with her teacher and the other students in her studio.

Whether inside or outside a conservatory, an individual's ability to perform musically is contingent on a sense of the social situation. For example, a question such as "What is music?" is probably less relevant to a young child's world-view than the question "What is music for me?" or, even more generally, "What does this sound pattern mean, or do, to me?" The knowledge of the types of behavior that are not appropriate to a youngster are every bit as important to that child's social competence as knowing behaviors that are appropriate. When musical performances result in rejection or ridicule, one response will be a strategic avoidance of comparable performances in the future.

A young child who grows up without acquiring competence in musical performance generally does so as part of a social process—one in which the child is indeed competent—of assimilating a somewhat generalized role of musical outsider. Taking such a role is a strategic response of a person whose performances have been systematically deprecated. In this connection it is worth calling attention to the very real social skills that are entailed in being a musically untalented person. A negative phrase such as "musically untalented person" calls attention only to a particular kind of deficiency, but such a person generally has an abundance of highly complex social skills in the negotiation of everyday life. By now it is pretty well accepted by social scientists that "the production of society . . . is always and everywhere a skilled accomplishment of its members" (Giddens 1976: 126), and being a musically untalented person is just as definitely a skilled social accomplishment as having talent. Indeed, talented musicians (and other "artistic types") are stereotypically awkward and out of place in many "normal" social environments, and make a significant contrast with people who can get considerable social mileage from professing, with great charm, of course, to have a "tin ear."[5]

The connection between the "verbal performance" and the "performative utterance" aspects of critical evaluation of a person's talent, of course, lies in the fact that it is the esteem derived from the skillful performance of verbal criticism and commentary that gives constitutive force to an attribution of talent. Since Jill's talent is attributed to her by Jack, the validity of her talent is contingent upon Jack's musical esteem. Jack's musical esteem is acquired, in part, through skilled performances of critical commentary.

This, however, closes off an analytical circle, for one element in Jack's stature as a critic is his savvy in assessing the musical talent of others. Once Jack has attributed musical talent to Jill, his continuing critical esteem will hinge in part on Jill's subsequent musical success. Not only is musical "talent" relational, but the social relations characterized by an attribution of talent link the esteem of the persons involved. When Jack says that Jill is very talented, his own esteem becomes tied in part to her social acceptance as a musical performer. If, subsequently, Jill's musicianship meets with general disapproval, such disapproval tends to be accompanied by observations that "Gee, Jack thought she was good—well, I guess that shows how much he knows." However, to the extent that Jack's esteem is beyond challenge, Jill's acceptance as a musician is made much more likely ("so what if Bill doesn't like her playing? What does he know anyway? Jack says she's talented").

An assessment of musicality or talent is not something that is ever proved or disproved. Rather, it is validated with reference to the same social process in which it first arose. An assessment of musical talent is an esthetic judgment. An esthetic judgment of musical performance is a statement that is evaluative of a person or persons. Here we see the full force of Leach's dictum, referred to in Chapter One, regarding the relationship between ethics and esthetics.

# The Parable of the Talents

The linking of esteem between the person attributed with talent and the person or persons making the attribution leads to an observation that bears on the positive value placed on being "talented," the notion that talent is a "gift" to be envied or coveted. The fact is that while being "talented" may be positively valued, it nevertheless entails definite moral obligations of musical development. A young person's talent is an attribution that demands development for the benefit of others as well as for oneself. The youngster who shows some talent in early years but declines to further this musical development is the bane of both parent and schoolteacher. Conversely, the demands made by expectant parents of their talented offspring are the scourge of many ambivalent music students, such as the Midland student discussed in Chapter One who thought it would not be permissible for her to major in oriental art "because I'm talented."

It is worth remembering that the concept of talent derives from the New Testament parable of the talents (Matt. 25: 14–30). This parable tells us that "a man going on a journey called his servants and entrusted to them his property; to one he gave five talents, to another two, to another one, to each according to his ability. Then he went away."[6] The parable makes a moral imperative of developing (investing) one's given talents in the absence of the master, but in connection with the sense of duty and obligation experienced by so many musically "talented" youngsters, it is hardly insignificant that the talents (units of money) in the parable are the property of the master and not of the persons charged with their care.[7]

This distinction can be of help in understanding the symbolic nature of musical talent in Western culture. With reference to the biblical parable, a musician's "talent" can be seen more as the "property" of a cultural ideology than as a "property" or characteristic trait of the individual person. Talent is no more the "property" of the musician to whom it is attributed than the monetary talents of the parable were the property of the servants to whom they were given. Once again, musical talent is attributed to certain people in certain situations, rather than being an a priori physiological property of the person.

There can be no escaping the fact that both the manifesting and the assessing of musical talent are to a great extent matters of social power and authority. The college-aged conservatory singing student performing in a promotional audition before an audience of highly trained and critical singing teachers (or in a recital before a collection of highly competitive fellow singing students, who, the performer may think, will be eager to pick up on any and all imperfections) nevertheless has a considerable store of resources in the situation. These resources include the support and encouragement from the student's teacher or studio clique, the student's general social maturity, and the music-technical and emotional preparations that the student has gone through in the days and weeks before the actual performance.[8] Although the student may well perceive a situation of adversity, that student nevertheless has considerable social and personal resources for dealing with the situation.

A small child, however, is likely to have no such resources. The youngster in the third-grade choir who is told to mouth the words but actually not to sing with the other children confronts a situation of relative adversity far greater than the not completely hypothetical conservatory student just described. Such a child generally has no way to combat such adverse conditions, and almost certainly has no way of knowing what might be done to improve the singing. What is wrong with the child's singing? Too loud? Too raspy? Off pitch? Not only does the child not know the answer to such questions, she or he is likely to be unaware that such questions exist. To the child, the only thing wrong with the singing is likely to be that she or he is the one who is doing it.

It is not a minor point to note that among adults who consider themselves to be untalented or unmusical, childhood experiences of this kind are a very common phenomenon indeed. Significantly, people who as children encountered such experiences are likely to report them only as evidence of their own complete nonmusicality: "I'm so bad, why, I couldn't even make the third grade glee club." The point here is that these persons' nonmusicality was socially developed in the context of social power relationships in which they were at an insuperable disadvantage.

Of course, some of these "untalented" people do in fact make music almost daily, although in a very constricted social environment where they are completely safe from possible adverse judgements. I refer here to such activities as humming while waiting for someone to come to the phone, whistling or toe-tapping with the radio and television, and the like. In a similar vein, I have a friend who has for years insisted energetically that she is totally unable to do anything that requires even minimal melodic or rhythmic competence, and the one time that she allowed me to try to help her, she was indeed unable to master some very simple musical patterns that I made up for her. Of late, however, she has become a mother, and several times recently I have heard her singing nursery tunes, with both confidence and competence, to her young daughter. Musical competence grows—or withers—in the context of particular social relationships.[9] On the other hand, social relationships are not autonomous, bounded entities. My friend's competence in singing is surely grounded in her own motherhood, but her baby is not the only person who has heard her sing, as is evidenced by that fact that I am writing about it. Whether or how her music making continues to broaden and develop will be contingent on various changing personal relationships, one but only one of which will be her relationship with her growing daughter.

This, of course, is simply another way of saying that social contexts are intercontextual. Underlying the observation that what is music for one person may be cacophony for another lies the fact that whatever transpires within the context of musical performance is evaluated and validated in a different context, in terms that derive their meaning and force from social considerations outside the performance event. If my music is your cacophony, or if someone I think is talented seems unmusical to you, we know this from having discussed it outside the recital hall. The reflexive behavior of the critical listener is pertinent here, since in mentally preparing evaluative commentary, a critical listener links the musical context to a conversational context. The conversational context, in turn, often brings the domain of music into the same context as various other social domains.

The very meaning of musical "talent" is inextricably linked to power relations. The concept is used in the context of marked differentials in social power (parent-child, teacher-pupil); ambiguities of its meaning are clarified through referral back to higher levels of this power structure; and perhaps most importantly, the invocation of "talent" contributes significantly to the reproduction of a structure of inequality in social power.

The simple fact that some people are "natural" musicians and other people are "tone-deaf" is neither as simple nor as natural as it sometimes seems. Musical "talent" is not God's truth, but neither is it hocus-pocus. Talent is a cultural symbol, which in this case constitutes a transformational link between the "political" and the "musical." An attribution of talent interprets musical expression in terms of the recruitment of an elite. It is an interpretation of perceived affective experience (she plays from the heart) in terms of social rank (she is unusual—it isn't just anyone who can do that). Moreover, an attribution of "talent" separates the value of a special social superiority from the value of individual choice, and not infrequently places these values in direct conflict with each other. Sometimes this conflict is acute and painful, but usually the special status is assimilated, and provides relief from the burdens of making what may be quite difficult choices.

What must be emphasized, however, is that an attribution of "talent" brings a positive value to a perceived social inequality. When Jack attributes musical talent to the young Jill, her values are affected along with her self-image. Many such young people willingly endure personal sacrifices in order to develop their musical talent. Occasionally, of course, someone will decline to develop the acknowledged talent, and in such a case the attribution is devalued, since obviously something else is more important. Here, however, important social forces (intimate relationships: parents, teachers, or friends) are brought to bear on the young person. The political tension of such a situation is not that of people competing over a scarcity of valued goods, but rather over a conflict of value and meaning. Such conflicts are generally negotiated on the basis of material conditions: the music lessons will be subsidized, but the youngster must develop other interests on his or her own.

# Cultural Polymorphism

Talent is a cultural symbol that is both *polysemous*, having multiple meanings, and *polymorphic*, having multiple manifestations. Its polysemy is seen in the variety of usage already discussed: talent as potential, as differentiation, as moral responsibility for development, and as intrapersonal immanence. These various meanings of talent receive differing emphases in different contexts and can be seen as at least occasionally mutually exclusive. The polymorphism of talent can be seen, for example, in the differences among piano playing, flute playing, and cello playing, enterprises that are so different from each other that it would be impossible to specify the traits of "talent" that are common to all. Such a problem would only be increased by adding singing to the list, or drum playing or tuba playing. Being a talented drummer entails a radically different set of responses and skills from being a talented pianist or singer.

The polymorphism of talent, however, goes far beyond the domain of music. "I think I have a talent for writing," a physical anthropologist said to me recently in explaining her choice of profession, and other scholars have said very similar things. Thus we have scholarly writing or teaching joining cello playing and singing as manifestations of talent. Making bouquets and floral arrangements can also be a manifestation of talent, at least to the person who referred to a neighbor who is "a very talented florist." Another area in which talent is manifested is sports: "If there's any such thing as 'natural talent,' Joanie's got it," says a high school basketball coach. "She has a nose for where the ball is going, plus she intimidates people defensively because she's so quick." Thus apparently being quick or intimidating, or having "a nose for where the ball is going" can also be manifestations of talent.

One might well wonder, since talent is manifested in flute playing, singing, violin playing, drumming, and piano playing, as well as in scholarly writing, flower arranging, and basketball playing, why more people don't interpret such diversity as inherently contradictory. It might well be taken as a point of common sense that a single phenomenon cannot simultaneously "be" drumming, singing, flower arranging, and basketball playing, so why don't people point to the polymorphism of talent as evidence that talent really doesn't exist, and isn't really real? If anything, there appears to be a tendency to do precisely the opposite, that is, to cite the infinite variety of manifestations of talent as corroboration of its reality (see? it's all around us, it's everywhere, it's natural!) rather than as evidence of internal contradictions.

The key to the polymorphic nature of talent is hinted at by the contingent "if" which began the coach's statement. Talent is a concept frequently used to explain something that couldn't be explained otherwise.[10] Like the concept of "a nose for the ball," the notion of talent in the coach's statement appears to be a somewhat figurative expression, used in an attempt to make manageably meaningful certain actions that cannot be described in sufficiently specific language to be taught formally.

It is worth noting, in this connection, that the conceptual congruence between one sense of "talent" (the sense contrasted with "technical proficiency") and that which cannot be taught is hardly random coincidence. By the same token, the prospect that everybody might be taught to do something implicitly entails an argument against the pertinence of "talent" to that enterprise. Thus we arrive at the paradoxical fact that musical talent is that which can't be taught to the few who can be taught it. To say this is not simply to play a trick with words, but rather to bring us to the seeming impossibility of rendering in words the essential nature of musical expression. In that "classical" music is an idiom that virtually by definition entails a very high quotient of formalized teacher/pupil relationships, relationships that in turn entail a great degree of verbalized instruction, the notion of talent can be seen as an ideological accommodation to the paradox of giving formal verbal instruction in a nonverbal idiom. The dynamics of talent in a formalized teacher/pupil context will be discussed in detail in the next chapter.

For all its polymorphism, there is an element of meaning common to all of these manifestations of talent, whether musical or nonmusical: a hierarchy of ranking in social skills. The various manifestations of talent, from cello playing to basketball playing, can be seen as manifestations of a single "thing," namely hierarchical inequality. Talent, in its countless manifestations, represents a cultural experience of inevitable, indeed natural, social hierarchy. And in spite of the seemingly fervently held "truth" that "all men are created equal," talent is very much a positive value in present-day Western culture.[11] As the wife of one conservatory alumnus expressed her congratulations for her talented husband's recent successes in his musical career, "cream rises."

The practise of interpreting divergent phenomena as manifestations of a single, unitary entity is one of the most important factors in the social reproduction of culture.[12] The analytical notion of polymorphism—whereby seemingly unitary cultural representations are seen to entail numerous divergent manifestations—pertains not only to the notion of talent, but also to the notion of music, not to mention countless other cultural representations. Conservatory musicians consistently distinguish between playing the music and playing the notes, and yet also insist that performers "play what the music says." Thus music, like talent, not only has numerous contexts but also numerous manifestations, some of which will be elaborated in the following chapters.

# LESSONS WITH THE MASTER

## A Distinguished Personage

As was noted earlier, I attended four classes at EMCM on a regular basis, in the hope that such a schedule would provide me with optimal opportunities to see the school while keeping my own obtrusiveness to a minimum. The primary criteria for selecting classes to attend were those of maximizing the types of students that I would be likely to observe on a regular basis. Thus, I selected one class for freshmen, one for graduate students, and two for upper class undergraduates. One of the latter was a class specifically for singers, the other a class for instrumentalists.

My selection for this latter category was a class in chamber music performance, and was of particular interest to me because of its renowned teacher, Marcus Goldmann. Goldmann is internationally famed both as a concert pianist and as a pedagogue. A former student of the legendary Artur Schnabel, he is a prominent scion in one of the most celebrated of music pedagogical lineages. While Goldmann's class did meet my criteria for optimal data gathering quite nicely, issues other than research validity also affected my selection of this class, since my own music pedagogical lineage includes another well-known member of the Schnabel "clan." Thus, although I attended all classes "as" an anthropologist, I selected Goldmann's chamber music class because it was one which I would enjoy attending "as" a piano student, as well.

Classes met once weekly, lasting three hours with two ten-minute intermissions. The students were divided into six small ensembles, with each hour of class being devoted to a lesson with one ensemble playing an assigned piece of repertoire; each ensemble could expect to play and be coached in class every other week. Goldmann sat facing the ensemble currently being coached; the remainder of the class was seated in the portion of the room nearer the doorway. With very few exceptions (such as myself), everyone in the room was enrolled in this class for academic credit, and thus while only one ensemble could play and be coached at a time, the other students were not simply an audience, but were also members of a class: ostensibly at least, Goldmann was teaching the entire class, and not only the ensemble presently being coached.

Goldmann's reputation as a teacher, a concert artist, and, at least secondarily, a prominent link in the Schnabel lineage extends beyond the confines of the conservatory community. Students have crossed a continent or an ocean specifically in order to study at EMCM with Marcus Goldmann. This fact alone gave Goldmann's presence in the classroom an important quotient of authority, and there can be no doubt that authority was a crucial aspect of his teaching.

One of the first things that I found noteworthy in this class was the exuberant intensity of Goldmann's teaching. As an ensemble played, he would be more or less constantly gesticulating with his arms and head, often singing or humming musical directives to the students. Several times during the period of my fieldwork I remarked to myself that in Goldmann's class I was getting "more data" than I got in other classes and rehearsals. The reason his teaching struck me that way relates to my "what is at issue?" guide question for observing conservatory interaction: the effect of the communicative intensity of Goldmann's teaching was to present his every phrase as a major issue.

Occasionally the issue for Goldmann was the attentiveness—or more precisely, the lack of it—of the class members not presently playing and being coached. The layout of the class was such that there was a considerable tendency for these students to experience themselves in the role of audience, or perhaps even as observer—bystanders, and thus as essentially immaterial to the progress of the class. Although Goldmann's energies and attention were sometimes so fixed on coaching the ensemble that he was unaware of the inattentiveness of the other students, he did occasionally direct his attention specifically to this matter. "What's that book you're reading?" he once demanded of a student in the back of the room. The student silently held the book up for Goldmann to see: *The Seven Storey Mountain* by theologian Thomas Merton. "That's a *good* book," said Goldmann in a voice which melded enthusiasm with sarcasm, concluding harshly, "now put it away!"

In addition to occasionally reprimanding students for their disruptions or inattention, Goldmann periodically directed analytical questions and comments to the audience portion of the class. "What was wrong with the way they did that? Anybody? Yes, Julie?"[1] It must be understood that in initiating this kind of class discussion, Goldmann had no intention of inviting subjective or impressionistic responses from the students. Goldmann always had a specific answer in mind, and such a discussion was rarely ended until his point was not only thoroughly explained but acknowledged (although sometimes only through lip service) by all members of the class.

# The Contingent Authority of the Musical Score

A fundamental principle of Goldmann's teaching was that students must play what is printed in the score, and yet that they must not play something simply because it is written in the score, but rather because they feel it that way. Part of the point here is that the score was of paramount importance, and the importance of the score was conceived by teachers and students alike as grounded in a devout respect for the creativity of the composer. However, everything happened as though the score were in its essence only a touchstone in an ongoing negotiation of relative social authority among the persons in the room, an authority manifested in musical and verbal performance.

To understand this point, it must be understood that although the authority of the score is paramount, it is hardly absolute. The authority of the score is contingent on a variety of factors, one of which is the authenticity of the edition presently in use. This authority is frequently impeached with reference to another edition of the composition, a version of the score that is held to be more authentic. The importance of this issue for Goldmann was several times manifested explicitly in class. Thus, when once a student reacted to one of his comments by saying, "But there are staccato marks over the quarter notes there," Goldmann rejoined by saying, "That score is not the original—those should be full quarter notes."

The question of the authenticity of a particular edition of the score is of major importance in present-day musical performance, and editions that include extraneous editorial markings—and there are many such editions, whose editors have introduced markings without distinguishing them from the original notations of the composer—are generally viewed with disdain by trained musicians. Here we touch on a concern that performers share with musicologists: an important focus of musicological scholarship has for some time been the enterprise of researching the manuscripts and original publications of the important composers, and publishing editions that are faithful to the thus legitimized and authenticated texts. While musicological research has established, to the general satisfaction of most academic musicians, a standard urtext edition for certain composers (perhaps the best example is the Bach Gesellschaft edition of the works of J. S. Bach), the relative authenticity of the various editions of the works of many nineteenth-century composers is an area of considerable professional controversy.

Once in a discussion over a cup of coffee, Goldmann told me some of his own views on the relative merits of some of the better-known editions. His remarks on editions of Chopin are significant here, even though no works of Chopin were studied in this chamber music class. He said that in contrast with other composers where there is a more or less clear-cut "definitive" or urtext edition, with Chopin one has to refer to several editions. He thought the Mikuli edition was the best. After all, he said, Mikuli was a student of Chopin (again evidencing the practise of validation with reference to pedagogical lineage). By contrast, he characterized the Paderewski editions as "lousy," mentioning with ridicule the occasional appearance of multiple "forks" (horizontal symbols indicating increase or decrease in loudness) going in contrary directions (Figure One).

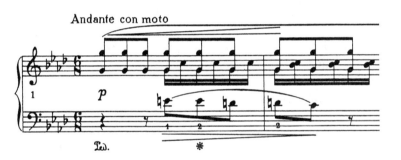

FIGURE ONE: an example from the Chopin Ballade in F Minor, as found in the Paderewski edition. Note the *crescendo* "fork" above the treble, and the *diminuendo* "fork" below the bass.

The matter of problematic indications in the score was frequently an important issue in Goldmann's class. His contempt for what he felt were absurd indications in the Paderewski editions of Chopin is at least somewhat ironic and is highly pertinent .o this discussion. For example, while coaching a duo on the Beethoven Sonata in C Major for cello and piano (opus 102 no. 1) he criticized the cellist's rendition of the opening phrase by directing his attention to the three Italian words in the text. "What markings are there?" he demanded of the student. Without having to refer to the score, the student was able to answer: *teneramente, dolce,* and *cantabile*. "Bravo," responded Goldmann, almost certainly forgetting that he had asked the same question of the same student a month earlier. "Now," he continued, "what does it *mean*?"

Waiting only for the first half syllable of the student's response, Goldmann seemingly changed the subject altogether: "what's it mean, the feeling of the second movement of the Beethoven C Minor Concerto? The score indicates *largo, pianissimo,* and to pedal through the harmonies." Goldmann motioned the accompanist aside and sat down at the piano. "There's a way to do this," he continued, adding somewhat parenthetically, "you need a really good piano to do it." He began to play, but interrupted his own playing: "a lot of people say that it sounds muddy if you hold the pedal down through all the changes of harmony," he said, "but it doesn't have to sound muddy. You have to cover the inside harmonies by voicing the bass and soprano lines." He played the opening of the concerto movement, keeping the damper pedal depressed throughout the phrase. "That didn't sound muddy, did it," he said, more as a boast than as a question. "It's *misty.*"

Several important points can be drawn from this episode. Goldmann was illustrating his view that problematic indications in the text, such as that for holding the damper pedal through several changes of harmony (generally considered unstylistic and even distasteful in playing tonal music), can lead the performer to a particularly insightful rendition of the passage in question. The context of his discussion of the opening of the Piano Concerto movement—a discussion of the three words at the beginning of the C Major Cello Sonata—brings into relief a point that Goldmann himself mentioned only in passing, namely that the solution to the problem posed by the unorthodox pedal marking is suggested by a consideration of other indications in the text: *largo, pianissimo*. Goldmann was unsatisfied with the way the cellist had played the opening phrase of the cello sonata, and his criticism was that the student had inadequately thought about how to simultaneously play *teneramente* (tenderly), *dolce* (sweetly), and *cantabile* (singing).

Goldmann's denunciation of the problematic markings in the Paderewski editions of Chopin have a particular significance in this context. Part of Goldmann's point regarding the Paderewski edition was that the opposed forks are self-contradictory—impossible to execute, and an esthetic absurdity. In this, however, he was saying something similar to what many musicians say about the pedal indication in the slow movement of the Beethoven C Minor Concerto, namely that the marking violates the canons of stylistic performance. The more basic point, then, is that the impossibility or absurdity of a given textual marking is in inverse relation to the perceived authority of the text edition in question. Goldmann's decrying the forks in the Paderewski Chopin edition was one and the same act as rejecting the authority of that text. His point to the class in playing the opening phrase of the piano concerto movement was to show that with an authoritative edition of a musical masterpiece, problematic indications in the score are not only unassailable but also invaluable. Honoring them is taken not only as always necessary, but also sometimes as sufficient for proper performance.

Lest this last statement be taken as even more sweeping than it was intended to be, it must be emphasized that the matter of what is and what is not in accordance with the dictates of the score, that is, what constitutes honoring the score in performance, is almost always problematic and frequently at issue among conservatory musicians. Goldmann's point about the cellist's rendition of the opening of the Beethoven cello sonata was that he was playing with an improper musical "feeling" and that he was being insufficiently attentive to the indications of the score. In turn, my point about Goldmann's teaching is that these two criticisms, improper feeling and inattention to the score, were with Goldmann effectively the same thing. Only in honoring the textual indications can one give the proper feeling to the performance, and, for the most part, only the performer who feels the music properly can honor such problematic textual indications.

The authority of textual markings—as authentic instructions from a musical creator—is systematically invoked by teachers and students alike, but it is also contested in a similarly systematic fashion. Goldmann impugns the Paderewski Chopin, while others might not. (Goldmann notwithstanding, many pianists take the Paderewski Chopin edition to be the most authoritative available.) Goldmann honors the long pedal marking at the opening of the second movement of the Beethoven C Minor Piano Concerto, while others clearly do not. What must be emphasized is that any edition of the score—that is to say, any real manifestation of the score—is but a passive resource and not an active agent in musical performance, or in negotiations of musical meaning, quality, and authority. While the score is invoked as an authority in Goldmann's class, it must be kept clear that the real authority does not reside in the score, but in Goldmann and, to varying extents, in the students. The authority of the score is contingent on musicological (printed or spoken) verifications of its authenticity and on "authoritative" performances perceived to be in keeping with the score's indications.

The rendering in performance of an authoritative musical text necessarily and inevitably raises questions of interpretive evaluation. Such evaluation, in turn, centers on the musical and affective feelings of the persons in question, in this case, of Goldmann and the students in the class. While a musical performance does have a relationship to the score, that relationship is in no way fixed, explicit, or determinate. On the contrary, the relationship between performance and score is fundamentally indeterminate and problematic.

As illustration of this latter point, it is significant that on at least one occasion Goldmann explicitly contradicted an indication given in the score, without casting doubts on the authenticity of the edition in use. "Janet, you don't use your ear," he complained to a student working on the Brahms horn trio. "Think of it as *pianissimo* rather than as *piano*." Moments later, as she played, he insisted, "*pianissimo*, play *pianissimo*!" Taken literally, it is clear that Goldmann has contradicted the text: the score says *piano*, Goldmann says *pianissimo*. Taken practically, however, the effect of Goldmann's comments was to clarify to the student the aural meaning of the Brahms *piano* indication.

Paradoxical as it may seem, Goldmann's invoking of the score as the paramount authority can itself be seen as part of a particular aural tradition; rigorous adherence to the score is unquestionably a hallmark of the Schnabel legacy that Goldmann inherits. One salient feature of Schnabel's legacy is the emphasis he placed, both as a performer and as a teacher, on conscientious adherence to the dictates of the score (Schonberg 1963: 404–408). Schnabel was an early and important representative of this twentieth-century approach to musical performance, in which tempo fluctuations or inflections conceived by a performing artist as "expressive" or as virtuostic elements in performance came to be viewed as "excessive" whenever not in accordance with the printed instructions of the score. At present, the general acceptance of this approach, stressing the paramount authority of the score, is unassailable: it is not only Schnabel disciples who profess such a doctrine. Nevertheless, Goldmann's consistent emphasis on the importance of the score can be taken in part as a representation of his Schnabel heritage.

A contrasting approach to the performer's attitude toward the score can be seen in a few comments I heard in the master classes of Saul Bernstein, whose violin pedagogy is perhaps even more renowned than Marcus Goldmann's piano teaching. Bernstein clearly felt that the problem of making a convincing performance occasionally obliges the performer to take certain liberties with the score. Of a bowing indication in the Mendelssohn Violin Concerto, he said, "that looks good on paper, but it will never work in performance. When you get out in front of the public, this is what it'll sound like." Whereupon he played the passage, bowing as indicated, in such a way as to sound awkward and stilted. Similarly, in a lesson on the Brahms Violin Sonata in G Major, Bernstein addressed himself to a certain part of the text, saying, "I know I'm wrong, but I just cannot feel it that way."

The analytic significance of Bernstein's "I know I'm wrong, but" can hardly be overemphasized. Bernstein was clearly saying that there are two domains of value, of rightness/wrongness, in musical interpretation: the score and the performance, each of which should ideally be taken as primary. Bernstein was well aware of the critical disdain that can be visited on performers who too cavalierly disregard the directives of the composer's text. His "I know I'm wrong" was an unambiguous gesture of deference to the supposedly ultimate authority of the score. At the same time, he was demonstrating that when the values of performance are perceived as conflicting with those of fidelity to the score, then good performance takes primacy over adherence to the score.

The dualism between score and performance is no less significant for an understanding of Goldmann's teaching, and Goldmann's more steadfast insistence on adhering to the directives of the score must not be taken to mean that he was in any way indifferent to the importance of compelling performance. Goldmann's lessons illustrated a belief that with an authentic edition of a work by an acknowledged genius, the values of good performance simply cannot conflict with adherence to the score.

In either case, it should be clear that the analytic distinction between textual and aural transmission of music is at most an imprecise one. A distinction between these categories should be conceived metaphorically in terms of a broken, or even dotted, line. The indeterminate relationship between these two domains is forcefully demonstrated by the teachings of Goldmann and Bernstein.

# The Importance of "Feeling" in Musical Performance

Unquestionably one of the most important features of Goldmann's teaching was his constant emphasis on feeling in musical performance. His insistent emphasis on the authority of the score notwithstanding, his teaching stressed that adherence to the score must never be literalist or slavish, but felt and enthusiastic. It should be remembered that in stressing the value of carefully studying the problematic indications in the text, his question was, "What does it mean, the feeling at the beginning of the slow movement of the Beethoven C Minor Piano Concerto, with the markings of *largo, pianissimo*, and pedal through the harmonies?" Honoring the score and playing with feeling were for Goldmann but two aspects of the same thing; each entailed the other. Once again, the student must do as the score directs, but not because she or he feels it that way. The meaning of the Italian words (*largo, pianissimo*) was not simply their English translations, but rather the sensibility the score required.

One important indication of the importance Goldmann placed on playing with feeling was his own high-energy participation in the lessons. As students played through a portion of a piece, he would typically nod his head, brandish his arms, and hum, grunt, or sing verbal directions. "Oohhh, ooh, oh, I wish you'd feel that harmony more," he said as a duo played the Brahms F Minor Clarinet Sonata. Urging the students in a Beethoven septet to generate a sense of motion in their playing, he said, "Make it go forward, there," and in another context, "Feel it intensely—*want* to go there, but *don't*."

Instructions such as these show Goldmann to be teaching by telling the students directly how to feel the piece, how to feel while playing particular passages. This was a frequently used device for Goldmann, and it shall not go without saying that in this he was referring to internal affective states. "Feelings," of course, are generally conceived as inner states of sensibility, emotion, or affect, and one meaning of the phrase "playing with feeling," as I have been using it, can safely be taken in this sense. However, Goldmann's attention to playing with feeling was not manifested solely in a concern with musical manifestations of internal states such as passion, calm, anxiety, foreboding, or exuberance. Playing "with feeling" frequently entailed perceiving the musical structures of the text in association with bodily motions—most notably of the hands and arms—and with the physical dynamics of singing and breathing.

One strategy frequently used by Goldmann was that of asking a student to sing a particular passage, an exercise that compels the student to experience a musical phrase in terms of a finite amount of exhaling breath, and to clarify beginnings and endings of phrases, experienced physically as points where a singer can inhale. When Goldmann told a young clarinetist to "take a breath, there" he was making a comment that was at once technical and interpretive, and he was doing this by giving a physical, bodily directive. Moreover, it was not only the players of wind instruments who were told to breathe or to "make it breathe" at phrase endings. Such directives were given to pianists and cellists as well, and the expression has become such a commonplace that its metaphoric character is in many cases lost. In many contexts, for a performer to "make it breathe" or for an ensemble to "breathe together" can be effectively synonymous with playing "with feeling."

This dialectical relationship between feeling as an internal affective and emotional state and feeling the bodily sensation of the inhaling and exhaling air is a crucial element in understanding the musical issue of playing with feeling. Goldmann's teaching, moreover, showed yet another facet of the notion of playing with feeling, one dealing with the motion and the weight of the hands and arms of the performer.

In coaching a pianist on the Beethoven Cello Sonata opus 102 no. 1, Goldmann showed clearly that particular arm movements could be understood as essential to the proper interpretation of the piece. "Play the unit technically as your impulse is," he said. Part of Goldmann's point was technical: the pianist should lift her hand away from the keyboard on playing the two sixteenth notes, and bring it down only by dropping on the accented quarter note that follows. At first she was keeping her hand close to the keyboard through the duration of the rest, then at his direction lifted her hand momentarily. Even then, however, she quickly returned it to the surface of the keyboard, from which distance she could be more certain of not hitting the wrong key. Goldmann's implicit point was that such caution was standing in the way of proper performance of the phrase. "If you don't do it with your hand," he said, "it won't get there." In other words, if she didn't lift and drop her hand around the eighth rest, the proper feeling of the phrase would not be projected (see Figure Two).

Here we have a case in which the value of note accuracy in musical performance competes directly with that of playing with feeling. Excessive attention to note-perfect performances was repeatedly criticized by Goldmann. "It's really fabulous that you can play all those notes, but I'm not interested in that," he once said to a pianist studying Beethoven's "Kreutzer" sonata. While wrong notes were of course never valued in and of themselves, it is clear that wrong notes in performance were frequently an at least unintended index of "expressive" playing. Moreover, technical imperfections could, it seems, themselves be valued directly. One of Goldmann's favorite comments to string players was "Let me hear some hair," a reference to the gritty or scratchy sound that comes from drawing the bow with great (or, stereotypically, "excessive") intensity.

Goldmann's admonitions to play with feeling were frequently verbalized in terms of the contrast between *technical* and *musical* aspects of playing. "Here's a technical problem," he would say. "How do you solve it?" The answer to such a question inevitably referred to a "musical" matter: "Very often, if you have a *musical* idea, it helps your *technical* control." The distinction between technical and musical aspects of performance is an all-pervasive concern among conservatory musicians, and the meaning of the contrast hinges on feeling. *Technique* refers to a performer's physical (bodily/motor) skill in controlling an instrument; it is conceived as though quantifiable (references are constantly made to people who "have a lot of technique") and at least metaphorically as substance, a thing in itself (for example, "technical equipment"). When contrasted with *musical*, the word *technical* refers to the absence of affective feeling or expression. A major thrust of Goldmann's teaching, however, was toward mediating this technical/musical dualism. His message was that not only must technique—in this case, configurations of movements of fingers, hands, and arms—be directed toward the goal of expressing musical feeling, but also that musical feeling could be an essential element of technique itself.

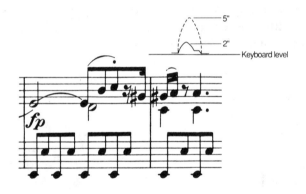

FIGURE TWO: an excerpt from Beethoven Sonata opus 102 no. 1. Dotted line curve schematizes the movement of the hand above the keyboard urged by Goldmann; the solid line curve represents the more timid movement of the student's (right) hand.

One passage where technical control was an issue in Goldmann's class is in the finale of the Brahms F Minor Clarinet Sonata. Goldmann pointed out that one difficult passage in the piano part could be made more manageable by feeling it in terms of three phrases in motion, rather than simply as an undifferentiated, extended succession of rapidly moving notes. Thus, in diametrical opposition to the stereotypical idea that performers must first learn the notes and then add the expression or feeling, Goldmann's position was that musical feeling was frequently essential to the technical mastery of the notes.

A frequently heard theme in Goldmann's class was that students should do what he said not because he said it, but because they felt it (thus inverting the age-old maxim of do what I say not what I do.) His conception for this was a distinction between what he said and what he meant. "Don't try to do what I tell you, try to express what I mean," he urged the students in one ensemble. To another group he said, "I told you to play it faster, now it's too fast. That happens with a lot of students. You know what I say more than what I mean." This, of course, was a way of chiding students for taking the directives of the score literally and slavishly, rather than with the appropriate feeling.

Clearly, Goldmann took the meaning ("express what I mean") of his own directives, as well as the meaning of indications in the text, to be the feeling engendered in effective performance. The concepts of "meaning" and "feeling" are here brought into such proximity that an attempt to make explicit distinctions between them would certainly lead away from an important point. For Goldmann and for his students, as well as for most musicians directly concerned with musical performance, the meaning of a piece entails the feeling that can be engendered in its rendition. The meaning of the markings at the beginning of the slow movement of the Beethoven concerto is the feeling that is aroused in their proper execution.

# Musical Meaning and Social Power

The thesis that meaningful social interaction is a skilled accomplishment of social actors has gained general acceptance in sociology and anthropology (Garfinkel 1967, Cicourel 1974, Giddens 1976, Bourdieu 1977). Inasmuch as the development of musical skills was the central focus of Goldmann's chamber music class, the pertinence of such a sociological thesis to Goldmann's class is striking: the skilled production of meaningful musical performance (which is, of course, a particular kind of social interaction) was, of course, the primary focus of Goldmann's course.

It should perhaps be mentioned, however, that among some conservatory musicians the issue of "meaning" in music is treated with considerable suspicion. For example, once in a conversation with a conservatory piano student I happened to ask if she was familiar with Leonard B. Meyer's *Emotion and Meaning in Music*. The student had never heard of Meyer's book, but she had evidently had experience with academic discussions of musical meaning, since she had a quick and intensely negative reaction to the title. She said that she hates to be told what to think and feel about a piece of music. "Everybody's got to do it themselves," she said. Her vehement comments reminded me of an earlier discussion, in which a pianist had reacted angrily to the suggestion that the final movement of Mozart's Concerto in C Major, K. 503, was "sad."

Such quasilinguistic conceptions of musical meaning are given extensive development in Deryck Cooke's *The Language of Music* (1959), in which particular melodic formulae are assigned specific affective significance (ascending intervals are "active," descending intervals "passive;" major intervals are joyful or optimistic, minor intervals tragic or pessimistic; hence, for example, a descending minor triad conveys "acceptance of, or yielding to grief . . . passive suffering" [Cooke 1959: 133]). Many musicians, however, take offense at suggestions that musical elements have "meaning" in any such linguistic sense. A suggestion that a Mozart concerto movement can be categorized as either "sad" or "happy" is very liable to bring the response that if music has meaning then that meaning is purely musical, and has nothing to do with sadness and happiness. One version of such a viewpoint was articulated by Igor Stravinsky, who said, "I consider that music is, by its very nature, powerless to *express* anything at all, whether a feeling, an attitude of mind, a psychological mood, a phenomenon of nature, etc. . . . If, as is nearly always the case, music appears to express something, this is only an illusion, and not a reality" (quoted in Cooke 1959: 11). Although some conservatory students might also feel uncomfortable with the unequivocal nature of Stravinsky's remark, there is nevertheless a feeling among many "classical" musicians that quasilinguistic conceptions of musical "meaning" serve only to diminish the importance of affective fantasy and feeling that comes from effective performance.

It is important here to clarify the distinction between these two rather general conceptions of "meaning." The one that is based on the linking of certain symbols with particular categories (whereby the word *tree* refers to a botanical category that speakers of French call "arbre," or whereby a descending minor triad in music is said to refer to "passive suffering") is not only widely accepted in American common sense, but is also often implicitly taken as the essence of what "meaning" *is*. It is such a conception of "meaning" in music that is treated with suspicion by many performing musicians. However, there is a second sense of the notion of "meaning," one that has been a major staple in the scholarly work of social scientists, namely meaning taken as the practical interpretation of ongoing social interaction. Taking meaning in this latter sense—the sense of musical "meaning" as perceived feeling in performance—meaningful music making is of utmost importance to everyone in the conservatory.

Moreover, the study of meaning in social interaction necessitates attention to relations of power, and issues of social power and authority were indeed salient in Goldmann's class, particularly in connection with the matter of playing with feeling. In this connection, it is important to expose the fallacy of treating power relations as though they were discrete or autonomous components of social interaction (Giddens 1979: 79ff., Adams 1975: 19). It is a mistake to think of power as though it were, for example, some form of quantifiable "juice" that flows through certain people in particular social contexts, as a substance capable of being transformed into verbal skill, musical skill, or artistic skill. It is illusory to think that a social skill (such as playing the piano) is one thing and any social power that may be associated with it is another. While the English language does have the two words, *music* and *power*, and while these two words do have unquestionably different meanings, it is nevertheless not correct to say that in a context of musical performances we have two distinct and separate phenomena, social power and performance skill.

Numerous studies have shown the importance of social power relations in skilled social action. Sociologist William F. Whyte's *Street Corner Society* (1955) includes a striking analysis of the relationship between social ranking and bowling ability. Whyte's study showed that men who were excellent bowlers during the week but who held low ranking in their neighborhood gang were systematically unable to bowl successfully against the gang leaders in their regular Saturday matches. At issue in such matches was rooting and cheering from the sidelines, and the strategic use of heckling by the members of the gang.

Sociolinguist William Labov found a similar phenomenon in his study of "sounding," a competitive verbal game common among inner-city American black youth. In this game of hurling "ritual insults" at protagonists in the group, Labov found that boys who were very good at "sounding" among themselves were unable to perform well when opposed by dominant group members (Labov 1972: 331). Both of these studies demonstrate a close interrelationship between social hierarchy and performance skills.

This can also be seen in Richard Bauman's discussion of the "emergent" character of social structure generated by skillful verbal performance:

> There is . . . a distinctive potential in performance by its very nature which has implications for the creation of social structure. . . . Through his performance, the performer elicits the participative attention and energy of his audience, and to the extent that they value his performance, they will allow themselves to be caught up in it. When this happens, the performer gains a measure of prestige and control over the audience— prestige because of the demonstrated competence he has displayed, control because the determination of the flow of the interaction is in his hands. (Bauman 1977: 43f.)

The studies of Whyte, Labov, and Bauman demonstrate the notion that social power and performance skill are closely interconnected. Power relations are clearly a constraint on social performance skills, but at the same time it is often skilled social interaction that reproduces relations of power. This fundamental tenet of Giddens' (1976, 1979) theory of social "structuration" was illustrated repeatedly and clearly in Goldmann's chamber music class. Musical performance skill could clearly be seen to be both product and producer of social power. At the same time, social power could be seen as alternatively a constraint on and a facilitator of musical performance skills.

Of particular interest in this matter are the clearly differentiating effects of Goldmann's teaching energy, energy that was, as has been already noted, of considerable intensity. After an ensemble had finished its rendition of the repertoire to be studied in a given lesson, Goldmann generally responded with a few phrases or sentences of highly generalized comments evaluating the performance just finished. The point of importance here is that sometimes these comments were highly laudatory, while other times they were disparaging "faint praise," if not downright deprecation. "Bravo, bravo, bravissimo," he might say, "you're so good I really don't want to say anything." Such a statement was not to be taken at face value, for after saying this, Goldmann would proceed to give the ensemble a very thorough and intense lesson, demanding a more "expressive" melodic inflection here, a different pianist's fingering there, or a more sudden change of tone quality in another place. Goldmann used the "I really don't have much to say" response to an ensemble's rendition on numerous occasions, but he said this only to indicate congratulation, praise, or encouragement; no ensemble rendition in class ever went without a thorough coaching from Goldmann.

The contrast of such praise with a tentatively uttered "excellent, um, excellent, some of it is excellent" should be clear enough, while less dramatic than that with "it sounds a bit flat," as spoken by Goldmann in a most dispirited tone of voice. Moreover, in the context of such skepticism from Goldmann, his aggressive manner of teaching—insisting on strict adherence to the score, on myriad minutiae of articulation, instrumental technique, and musical expression—frequently made the matter of playing with feeling problematic at best and impossible at worst. One student in the class told me that Goldmann had a "killer instinct" for getting and keeping the upper hand in interactions with the students. "Did you notice how he went after the pianist in that trio, to frustrate her and make her feel inadequate when she couldn't play a certain passage?" he complained. Another student, an undergraduate pianist who had clearly been perplexed by some of Goldmann's comments to her on the previous day, told me that she felt that some of his remarks had been "destructive," and clearly felt that he had been unfairly comparing her with the doctoral student pianist of the group that had performed before her.

In the context of praise such as "you're so good I don't want to say anything," Goldmann's coaching gave incentive for musical growth to already gifted students. However, the similarly intense coaching given to other students, when prefaced by remarks such as "it sounds kind of flat," were likely to be experienced as "destructive," "frustrating," or otherwise inhibiting and deleterious. The similarity between this effect of Goldmann's teaching and the impact of social pressures on the bowlers in Whyte's street corner gang is unmistakable.

The implications of this aspect of Goldmann's teaching deserve special discussion. It should not be glossed over that some students, such as the one who complained of Goldmann's "killer instinct," actively dislike Goldmann, finding him gratuitously abrasive. This same student, however, also acknowledged that Goldmann frequently had brilliant insights into the performance of chamber music, and in this, too, his view point was representative. Virtually nobody interpreted the gruffness of Goldmann's personality as inherently antimusical. And indeed, many other students quite like him: "His teaching is completely selfless, and yet also completely him," was the way one student voiced her admiration of Goldmann. The fact is that the culling of students perceived as less talented, less accomplished, or less "musical" is generally accepted as necessary and inevitable in conservatory life, even if this is accomplished in an unpleasant fashion. When, in a discussion with another conservatory piano teacher, I said that it was my impression that Goldmann went harder on the mediocre students than he did on the "star" students, the quietly prompt reply was, "Well, that's okay, that has to be done."

Goldmann himself was well aware of his image as a stern and unyielding personality; however, it seems clear that he saw this as a by-product of his resolute commitment to the highest of musical standards. Goldmann's pedagogical eyes were fixed on the Grail; the gruff treatment that was accorded to the students must be understood as an extension of his own sense of artistic commitment. The idea was that the music would be ill served by letting the lesser students have an easier time of it.

In the conservatory, musical performance and rendition are inextricably intertwined with the negotiation and reproduction of social inequality. The reproduction of a hierarchy, or perhaps more generally, a social diversity, in a particular cultural knowledge and competence must be taken as an integral element in the meaning of musical performance. When Goldmann told a group of students that their playing sounded "*so* matter of fact," he was saying both that (1) their skills in performance were clearly below acceptable standards (thus confirming the social hierarchy), and at the same time that (2) a hypothetical audience would in all likelihood find little of "meaning" in such a performance.

Thus, while playing with feeling is at the core of the meaning of musical performance, it must be emphasized that this is so only as this feeling mediates the social power relations that exist in musical performance situations. The free play of fantasy and imagination, of playing with feeling, are never "free" in musical performance. Musical feeling mediates social relationships, including the elements of power in those relationships, which constitute the situations of musical performance.

# Music, Performance, and Structure

Anthropologists are appropriately fond of debating the nature and the locus of various key theoretical concepts. The anthropological literature is filled with questions of whether modalities such as social structure, culture, or ideology truly exist in the thoughts and actions of the people under study, or are in reality only the explanatory constructions of the anthropologists. To me it seems only appropriate that similar questioning be applied to notions of music, as well as music structure and musical meaning. This is because most of the dominant scholarly notions of music, musical structure, and musical meaning have their basis in the stillness of musical texts, and most notions of musical structure are premised on an expressed contrast between music and performance.

In spite of the seeming concreteness of the term *structure*, it should be kept in mind that the widely accepted notions of musical structure are both doubly abstracted (structure is abstracted from music, which in turn is abstracted from performance) and idealized. The fundamental importance of the contrast between music and performance can hardly be overemphasized, and will be discussed again in Chapter Six. For the moment it should suffice to say that formal models of musical "structure" are characteristically produced by scholars who more or less exclusively study musical compositions, and that compositions are, at bottom, abstractions, or texts, and silent.[2]

The fact is, however, that musicologists and music theorists are many, and models of musical structure are hardly uniform. While there may be consensus that, for example, a certain chord "is" a $I_4^6$ chord, there may well also be disagreements as to whether that chord "really" constitutes a tonic harmony or a dominant harmony. There may also be disagreements regarding whether a certain passage has modulated to, say, the submediant, or whether the composer was "really" only using some "secondary dominant" chords to harmonically emphasize the submediant. Nor is there always consensus regarding what musicians call the "form" of a composition: there is room for disagreement, for example, as to whether Liszt's Piano Sonata in B Minor is in one movement or in three. It is both in spite of and because of such ambiguities of musical structure that structural elegance can be so frequently suggested, even if implicitly, as the ultimate basis of the magnificence of "classical" music. A performer simply cannot—and must not try to—"bring out" every structural element of a composition.

The open-ended interpretive problem of which structural elements should be "brought out" in a musical performance is one that relates to Marcus Goldmann's frequently heard remark that "music is better than the best possible performance of it." Goldmann's aphorism is a forceful way of characterizing the distinction between music and performance, and amply demonstrates the idealized nature of the music concept. Moreover, even though some musicians disagree with Goldmann's articulation (a position associated with his teacher Artur

Schnabel), there can be no mistaking the fact that it is musicians' differing ways of performing, their varying ways of invoking and appealing to musical structure—phrase length, organization into formal sections, harmonic, contrapuntal, and metric patterning, and so forth—that determine social relations in the conservatory. Differences on such matters among experts, however real and consequential, are as nothing when compared with the variety in conceptions of musical organization among learners. Indeed, this is arguably the most fundamental underlying social reality in the conservatory: the changing and differential command that people have over musical structure and organization, as these differentials are worked out in verbal and musical performance.

Conceived with reference to resources that are variable among performers, musical structure becomes a central element in the very social configurations that music itself is frequently thought to transcend. In Marcus Goldmann's class, to play the music (rather than, as he occasionally put it, to play the notes) entailed playing with feeling, in which a mastery of the composition was seen to be contingent in part upon the social relationships impinging on the performance. Musical structures, then, can be understood as both medium and result of meaningful social interaction.[3]

Such a position is congruent with what Holy and Stuchlik (1981) called "the structure of folk models," that is, the differential distribution, within a group of people, of interrelated ideas as well as the varying skills in manipulating or implementing these divergent notions. By contrast, such a viewpoint is diametrically opposed to the idea of musical structure in which it is taken to be simultaneously (1) the fixed, underlying essence of music, (2) fundamentally asocial or extrasocial (with anything of social character being labeled "extramusical") and (3) exclusive of musical performance.

I suspect that I would get no contention from "classical" music theorists for saying that musical structure entails a configuration of parts of constituent elements. Where the present notion of musical structure diverges from others is in the idea that the parts or elements of a musical structure include personal, human, and social elements.

Musical structure in the present sense entails a configuration of persons. One such configuration can be seen to be centered on Marcus Goldmann. This configuration entails the relations between him and his students, his association with his famous bygone mentor, as well as the ambiguous yet crucial authority of the musical text or score. While it is of course true that a score is not a person and thus that the configuration is not solely one of persons, it is worth remembering that the importance of the score is linked to a perception of the composer who, however lionized or canonized, once was a person (the late Mr. Beethoven, the late Mr. Brahms), and that the perceived authority of the text is in part a manifestation of respect.

Another sense in which my conception of musical structure differs, rather fundamentally, from the conceptions that occupy music theory textbooks is in emphasizing the processual, active, and developing nature of a sociomusical configuration. By virtue of being conceived as essentially extrasocial, the standard notions of musical structure are for the most part fixed and motionless, even while attempting to account for time and motion in terms of rhythm or meter. By contrast, the sociomusical configuration in Marcus Goldmann's class was one that was itself in a state of gradual but unmistakable progression. Students' musical skills were confirmed and challenged, developing and changing, in a variety of ways; Goldmann's pedagogical urgings were at times extraordinarily insightful and beneficial to the students; at other times his gruffness had an unmistakably deleterious impact on students' self-confidence and performance skill. In all of this, however, the crucial point is that in so doing, Goldmann was not being antimusical—on the contrary. Once again, the music would be ill-served by treating the less skilled students more gently.

To put all of this a bit differently: the study of music in contexts of performance and rendition suggests the conclusion that "music" doesn't "have" meaning, but rather that music is *given* meaning in performance. By the same token, the study of music in performance brings with it the realization that "music" doesn't "have" structure, so much as it is given structure in performance. Musical structure is not a phenomenon that leads its own existence outside of social action; rather, it is a notion that is variously invoked, appealed to, or cited in the context of social action.

Musical meaning is a social meaning, and musical structure a social structure. Relations of systematized social power—for example, those between Marcus Goldmann and his students—structurally constrain or facilitate manifestations of "feeling" in musical performance. Social relations are integral to the meaning of musical performance. Musical meaning is both product and producer of structures of social power relationships. Musical performance (including in this the social relations obtaining in performance situation: relations of power), musical meaning, and musical structure are linked in a nexus in which each aspect is both product and producer of the others.

# A SONG IN A STRANGE LAND

## The Recitals

A full-length public solo recital is a basic requirement for most undergraduate and graduate degrees from the conservatory. The senior or master's recital in the conservatory is academically comparable to a baccalaureate or graduate thesis in other academic disciplines. It is a major single undertaking that represents, in a sense, the summation of the student's musical development to date. The repertoire to be performed on the recital is the object of intense preparation that in most cases lasts several months, and sometimes the better part of a year. These recitals characteristically take place during the final semester of the student's degree program, and thus constitute individualized precursors to the students' graduation exercise. Each spring, the conservatory concert calendar is so filled with student degree recitals that not only are the evening and weekend times fully scheduled, but some students end up performing on weekday afternoons.

Not surprisingly, these recitals are anticipated by many of the students with great trepidation, an apprehension that was evidenced in an interesting way in the first weeks of my stay at the conservatory. I had originally wanted to do a series of interviews with students readying themselves for their recitals, but as I began setting up the interviews, I was told by several students that although they would be very happy—some of them seemed almost eager—to do an interview with me, they wanted to wait until after their recital. The impending recital was an ominous specter for them, and discussing it directly with a newly arrived researcher was clearly felt to be threatening.

The recitals took place in one of two smaller halls at either end of the conservatory building. In most instances, a degree recital entailed a reception in honor of the performer, and very often the people entering the hall went past a table in the foyer set out with wine and cheese, or cakes and coffee, for the reception that was to follow the recital. Once when there was no reception in the foyer there was a sign placed in a music rack at the door to the auditorium, inviting the audience to a reception at the performer's home a few miles from the conservatory.

The audience at these recitals varied greatly in size, ranging from as few as barely a dozen to as many as over two hundred. Typically, the larger audiences were drawn by local students who have a following of nearby family and friends. Other things being equal, the audience tended to be larger at recitals by students who were reputed in the conservatory to be leading performers, and at recitals where the "standard" solo repertoire would be performed: piano, cello, violin, or voice recitals generally drew more listeners than trumpet, bassoon, tuba, or percussion recitals.

The performer generally stayed invisible to the public while the audience gathered for the recital. As a rule, the audience gradually filed through the auditorium doors to await the beginning of the performance. The isolating of the performer from the public—which for some had begun with their unwillingness to discuss their recital preparations with me a few weeks earlier—was now emphasized visually by the emptiness of the stage. One deviation from this pattern occurred when the audience was kept outside the auditorium doors by the attendants while the performers engaged in some last-minute rehearsing of a violin and piano sonata. Although this last-minute onstage rehearsing did constitute an exception to the norms of recital activity, the fact that the audience was held outside behind closed doors confirms the more general point regarding the importance of keeping a distance between the audience and the performer.

Ostensibly, the tradition of keeping the performer backstage serves to enable the audience to enter and get settled in the auditorium without distracting the musician, that is, to facilitate the performer's concentration. However, in cases where the audience consisted of only a handful of friends and family, the tradition of keeping the performer invisible in this way surely served only to intensify the emotions of what was in effect a ritual event. In the smaller audiences, the only persons in attendance who were probably not themselves performing musicians were the soloist's own family members. Thus the members of the audience knew intimately, just as I know from my own experience as a performing pianist, the fears that can occupy a performer waiting backstage in anticipation of the moment to walk out onto the platform.

It was the smaller audiences that put the ritual character of the recitals most strikingly into relief. When the attendance consisted only of the performer's parents, teacher, and a few other students of the same instrument or perhaps even of the same teacher, its "public" character was compromised considerably. The people once assembled in the auditorium tended to keep virtually silent, speaking only in low whispers. A hush would last not only while the performer was actually playing, but would resume after the applause and for the most part last through the one- or two-minute intervals between pieces when the performer went offstage. Similarly, although people would leave the auditorium to talk during the intermission, within the recital hall a near silence was often effected spontaneously. In this very significant sense, these people were participating in a ritual as much as they were attending a performance.

The ritual quiet at these recitals was put into relief by the extraneous noises that intruded into nearly every recital I attended at the conservatory. Whether a fire alarm or siren from the city streets outside, a rehearsal organ heard through the ceiling of the concert hall, or a group of junior high school youngsters barging into the auditorium in mid-sonata, such noises shared one social trait: they were heard by all, but acknowledged by none. I was at one recital in which the melancholy quiet of the slow movement of Beethoven's *Das Lebewohl* Sonata (opus 81a) was forcefully violated by the sudden loud clanking of radiator pipes, and yet neither the performer nor the audience members betrayed any visible or audible evidence that this cacophony had had the slightest impact on the performance. Often when a performer came to a momentary silence in a piece (such as at the end of a sonata movement) there was a noticeable drone of extraneous sound—sound that was surely the more noticeable by virtue of the striking attempt at silence made by the audience.

A different kind of extraneous noise occurred during a gala concert featuring honored students of the graduating class, presented immediately prior to the conservatory's commencement exercise. One of the performers played a portion of a concerto for harpsichord and orchestra, something that, like most of the repertoire performed at this concert, necessitated the commotion of rearranging the orchestra, and in this case placing the harpsichord at the front of the stage. Once these arrangements were accomplished, the concert hall quieted, and the audience applauded as the soloist and conductor came on stage to begin the performance. It quickly became apparent, however, that the harpsichord was poorly adjusted, and throughout the concerto, the mechanical action of the instrument was so noisy as to nearly drown the harpsichord's music. The soloist tried to take advantage of a tacit passage in the piece to make the necessary adjustment on the instrument, but to no noticeable avail.

After the performance, the soloist inconspicuously joined the audience, where I happened to overhear her verbalize her considerable frustrations with the mechanical difficulties. Nevertheless, once the performance had begun, stopping it for the purpose of adjusting the harpsichord was clearly taboo. Although a few minutes of adjusting the harpsichord would almost certainly have facilitated a more satisfactory rendition of the concerto, stopping in the middle of the performance in order to do this would have violated something that was obviously experienced as even more basic: the ritual frame of the performance. Clearly, the emotional charge that inheres in the ritual frame of the event is experienced as both temporally and normatively prior to affective response to the melodies, harmonies, and rhythms of the performance. The ritual frame of a formal musical performance has its own emotional content, both for the audience and for the performer. This frame is a first element of the esthetic impact of a musical performance.

# Performance, Ritual, and Social Distance

In the previous chapter, the notion of *rendition* was suggested as a complement to that of performance, since among conservatory musicians, *performance* usually refers specifically to formally framed events in which music is played or sung before an audience. By contrast, among many anthropologists and ethnomusicologists, the notion of "performance" tends to be used to refer inclusively to any and all manifestations of the social making and doing of music. The music making in Marcus Goldmann's class constitutes performance in the sense used in social science discourse, although the people in the conservatory would not generally characterize what transpired in Goldmann's class as performance.[1] The present chapter deals mainly with performance in the sense used by conservatory musicians themselves, that is, with concerts and recitals.

A solo music recital is a ritual. It is a ritual in that it is a formally framed event in which one person is separated from the others with the imposition of an emotionally charged or sacralized social distance, namely, the separation between performer and audience. A solo recital is a ritual of individual accountability, in which the primary issue is whether the recitalist can display both the advanced technical training and the social decorum appropriate to the performer's role, all while giving evidence of a genuinely intimate interpretation of musical texts, which themselves can to a great extent be viewed as "sacred."

The title of this chapter refers metaphorically to the social distance that separates the performer from the audience, a distance that characteristically engenders considerable stage fright. The allusion is to the Old Testament account of the imprisonment of the Israelites at the hands of the Babylonians, and to the difficulty of singing in the context of such a hostile environment.

> By the rivers of Babylon, there we sat down, yea, we wept, when we remembered Zion. We hanged our harps upon the willows in the midst thereof. For there they that carried us away captive required of us a song; and they that wasted us required of us mirth, saying, Sing us one of the songs of Zion. How shall we sing the Lord's song in a strange land? (Psalms 137: 1–4)

This quotation provides a metaphoric reference point for understanding the stage fright felt by the soloist at a formal recital. Although it would be an overstatement to suggest that walking on stage to perform in a recital hall is comparable to being a prisoner of war, there can be no questioning the fact that the social distance that during a formal performance separates a recitalist from his or her audience tends to present the audience in a threatening if not hostile character. The allusion to the military conditions depicted in the Bible is corroborated by the words of one medical researcher who tested a drug for the control of stage fright in musicians: "a performer, beset by fear, finds his body reacting as it would when facing a hostile mob or a tiger."[2]

Having said this, it is worth pointing out that neither this kind of social distance nor the emotion of stage fright is in any way a universal experience of music making, even within Western cultural traditions. Different social forms of music making, such as group singing and playing to accompany group dancing, engender no such experience of stage fright. Indeed, the polar opposite to the despairing "how shall we sing the Lord's song in a strange land?" can be seen in an early American hymn that manifests a spiritual and political state of affairs radically different from that of the imprisoned Israelites of Psalm 137:

> No storm can shake my inmost calm
> While to that rock I'm clinging
> Since love is Lord of Heaven and Earth
> How can I keep from singing?
> When tyrants tremble when they hear
> The bells of freedom ringing
> When friends rejoice both far and near
> How can I keep from singing?

# Ritual in the Cult of the Individual

The teachers and students of the conservatory would, I feel certain, accept my designation of degree recitals as rituals, although perhaps in a way that would distinguish solo piano recitals from liturgical rituals such as Christian Communion, or perhaps from legal rituals such as swearing an oath in a court trial. They are completely aware of the highly formalized and patterned nature of the social behavior that takes place at senior recitals, although there is considerable ambivalence among many musicians regarding the nature—or in some cases, the existence—of any sacred element in conservatory recitals. "Music comes from God," said the oboe student. "Well, maybe not God, I'm not sure I believe in God, but. . . ."[3]

In interpretive social science, the use of the notion of ritual has traditionally entailed contending with the object of the ritual activity, which is to say, generally, with the problem of sacred values. Erving Goffman, one major sociologist who has theorized on ritual and individualism, honors this analytic tradition in his *Interaction Ritual*, which is a study of what he calls "face-to-face interaction in natural settings" (Goffman 1967: 1). In the chapter "On Face Work," Goffman discusses the various ways in which people maneuver to "save face" or to score "points" in everyday social interaction. This includes avoiding risky or uncertain situations, and explaining away social mishaps as unintended or insignificant; at issue also are such strategies as fishing for compliments or employing snubs and putdowns in conversation. Goffman defines "face work" as "actions taken by a person to make whatever he is doing consistent with face," (1967: 12), which is in turn defined as "the positive social value a person effectively claims for himself" (1967: 5). This may appear to be secular stuff indeed, and yet Goffman supports his characterization of ritual with reference to the notion of the sacred.

> I use the term *ritual* because I am dealing with acts through whose symbolic component the actor shows how worthy he is of respect or how worthy he feels others are of it. . . . One's face . . . is a sacred thing, and the expressive order required to sustain it is therefore a ritual one. (1967: 19, emphasis original)

The ritual aspects of a solo piano recital differ radically, of course, from those of apologizing for a social faux pas, and the sacralized nature of the role of soloist in a recital is quite different from the sacred qualities of what Goffman calls "face." In both of these, however, there is an adherence to the received wisdom of cultural analysis: understanding ritual has traditionally required an examination of that which is held as sacred. Such, in essence, is the position put forward long ago by Durkheim:

Rites can be defined and distinguished from other human practises, moral practises, for example, only by the special nature of
their object. A moral rule prescribes certain manners of acting to
us, just as a rite does, but which are addressed to a different class
of objects. So it is the object of the rite which must be characterized, if we are to characterize the rite itself. Now it is in the
beliefs that the special nature of this object is expressed. It is possible to define the rite only after we have defined the belief.
(Durkheim 1965 [1915]: 51)

Goffman elsewhere (1967: 47, 1971: 62ff.) links his theoretical formulation to the Durkheimian notion of the sacred individual, but however insightful Goffman's approach may be, it is significantly at variance
with Durkheim. As Goffman himself readily admits, saving one's face
often comes at the expense of injuring someone else's face, a fact that
raises important problems regarding the collective nature of the sacred
so central to Durkheim's formulation. Not only is Goffman concerned
with ritual elements of individual action, his very conception of ritual
is, at least on occasion, itself centered on the individual:

Ritual is a perfunctory, conventionalized act through which *an
individual* portrays *his* respect and regard for some object of ultimate value to that object of ultimate value or to its stand-in. . . .
In contemporary society rituals performed to stand-ins for
supernatural entities are everywhere in decay, as are extensive
ceremonial agendas involving long strings of obligatory rites.
What remains are brief rituals one individual performs for and
to another. . . what remains, in brief, are interpersonal rituals.
(Goffman 1971: 62–63, emphasis added)

The diction with which Goffman makes his case for the ritual character of "face work" provides a key to this point. For Goffman it is *one's*
face which is sacred: Goffman's notion of the sacred is grounded in the

concrete, experiencing individual, a conceptualization having a highly problematic relation with the Durkheimian notion of collective representations. It is important to remember that for Durkheim (1938: xlix), "the states of the collective consciousness are different in nature from the states of individual consciousness; they are 'representations' of a different type." Similarly, "the social fact is a thing different from its individual manifestations" (Durkheim 1938: 7). There is an important difference between the abstract Durkheimian notion of the collective representation of the individual, and Goffman's more concrete and egoistic notion of the social individual.

Goffman's face-saving ritual confirms the sacred character of the concrete, individual self. A solo recital, however, ritually reinforces abstract and collective ideas of individualism. This pertains quite directly to Durkheim's contention that collective and anonymous representations are both expressed and strengthened in ritual action (Durkheim 1965 [1915]: 245–255). A solo recital ritualizes the social distance between the performer and the audience. What is ritually enacted in all cases is the conceptual split between the individual and collectivity.[4]

A comment is in order, however, regarding the somewhat diffused sense in which I am using the term *sacred* in connection with social individualism and solo recitals. While I would hold that the collective representation of moral individualism is appropriately called "sacred," I find unacceptable another, seemingly self-evident, aspect of the Durkheimian formulation, namely that the sacred is by nature fundamentally opposed to the profane. The individual is sacred in contemporary Western culture, not so much in a sense that contrasts the individual with other, "profane," social configurations, but more in a sense that contrasts the sacred individual with contrasting or competing conceptions of the sacred. Goffman appears to be in error in equating his own conceptions of ritual and the sacredness of the individual with those of Durkheim (Goffman 1967: 47), but his formulation does suggest the value of an analysis that includes the possibility of simultaneous yet competing conceptions of the sacred in social action.

Moreover, the fundamental importance that in everyday life is placed on the person as an individual does not therefore make individualism a fundamentally secular or profane phenomenon. The idea that everyday life in Western culture is essentially secular is all too closely tied to the ethnocentric idea that it is "primitive" societies that are characterized by a pervasive concern with religion, the sacred, and the supernatural. Such a conception surely stands in the way of an anthropological understanding of religion both in modern Western culture and in those other cultures that have traditionally been the subject of anthropological inquiry. The world is not, as Durkheim held, divided into "two domains, the one containing all that is sacred, the other all that is profane" (Durkheim 1965 [1915]: 52), but rather into a plethora of domains in which distinctions between sacred/secular dualisms are either understood implicitly or contested and negotiated with reference to a variety of social contingencies.

The problem of the interpenetration of the sacred and secular domains can be seen in connection with Clifford Geertz's attempt to clarify the distinction between the "aesthetic perspective" and the "religious perspective." In the aesthetic perspective, according to Geertz, "instead of questioning the credentials of everyday experience, one merely ignores that experience in favor of an eager dwelling upon appearances, an engrossment in surfaces, an absorption in things, as we say, 'in themselves'" (Geertz 1973: 111). If this is the case, then the audience members at a conservatory recital are decidedly *not* taking an aesthetic perspective, since they are concerned with perceiving the essences behind the appearances. Members of a recital audience attend to the performance as an indicator of the inner musical makeup, the talent, of the person performing. It is the relative presence or absence of a performer's inner musical essence, or talent, that is at issue in a conservatory recital. In this, I would submit that the members of a recital audience partake of what Geertz tentatively called the "religious perspective." "The basic axiom underlying what we may perhaps call 'the religious perspective' is everywhere the same: he who would know must first believe" (Geertz 1973: 110). In other words, one who would fully appreciate a solo recital must belong to a cult of individualism; one must believe in the sacred importance of individual differences, in talent and in its importance.

A more dialectical relationship between the sacred and the secular in contemporary American culture might be illustrated with the suggestion that the belief in the primacy of a secular state (as manifested, for example, in the constitutional separation between church and state) is itself a sacred principle. The notion of a person as a morally autonomous individual may seem commonplace enough in everyday American thought, but it is clearly not a simple, objective fact of American political life, where, for example, a business corporation can for various legal and governmental purposes be considered a "person," and where inequities of various governmental systems are such that it is obvious that many individuals are not accorded rights supposedly granted to all persons. The notion of the person as moral individual is a highly ambiguous abstraction that has different implications in various contexts, many of which are simultaneously commonplace and sacred. A solo recital is one context in American culture that ritualizes—and renders sacred—an aspect of individualism. In such a context, it is the moral or artistic sensibility of the individual, rather than Jehovah, that metaphorically corresponds to "the Lord" of Psalm 137.

Nevertheless, labeling a solo recital a rite in a cult of the individual is a quite different matter from saying that John Doe's senior recital is a ritual in a cult of John Doe. Even if John Doe's recital were relatively unsuccessful—worse yet, embarrassing—for John Doe, the failures of a particular performance do not in the least compromise the ritual efficacy in strengthening adherence to the cult of the individual. On the contrary, the ritual efficacy of a solo recital is evidenced not only whenever success is described with reference to transcending the difficulties of formal performance (such as stage fright or unfamiliar surroundings), but also whenever failures are explained as being caused by those same difficulties. The issue is not just whether a person can play, what she or he can do at home or in the practise studio, but more what she or he can do in a recital.

The solo recital shows not only the opposition between Durkheim's collective and Goffman's egoistic conceptualizations of the sacred individual but also illustrates their interdependence. A senior recital in the conservatory is a "ritual" pertaining to a "sacred" individual in the sense of Goffman's formulation as well as Durkheim's. It is in a recital that the relationship between the concrete individual and the collective representation of individualism is most intense and uncertain. Western culture has few occasions in which the self, the ego, or the "face" are more directly threatened and endangered, and yet at the same time few occasions in which it is offered a more immediate source of potential gratification and fulfillment. Continual failure (or consistent success) by each and every John Doe who performed in a solo recital would obviously negate the efficacy of the recital as ritual in the (collective) cult of the individual. It is the variety of individual successes and failures that keeps the collective ritual meaningful. A given John Doe's recital must occasionally be a rite in a cult of John Doe as well as a rite in the more collective cult of the individual, but other recitals must bring some form of reproach on the performer in order that this ritual form maintain its efficacy. In the cult of the individual, to "sing the Lord's song" is to make a song one's own—to sing from the heart, or to sing with feeling. To "sing the Lord's song in a strange land" is, in such a way, to transform a threatening audience into an admiring following. The continuing efficacy of the recital as a ritual in such a "cult" requires that some, but not all, succeed.

# Individualism and Role Performance

One of the primary beliefs of the "cult of the individual" is the idea that the most important cultural accomplishment and economic productivity come from an individual acting on his or her own, independent and unaided. Stated differently, a primary belief of this cult is in the paramount importance of differentials of talent, a belief that the socioeconomic system should be structured in order to provide each individual with the productive niche that is particularly appropriate to that person's abilities. As was made clear in Chapter Three, such beliefs are closely linked to perceptions of social hierarchy as meritocracy, that is to say, to the idea that people attain power and authority because they deserve it, because they're better—because the cream rises.

Integral to this idea, however, is a factor of status indeterminacy, manifested in the fact that social and economic statuses are not only attained but also maintained through skilled performance. In a valuable discussion of the problematic character of status and role, sociologist Aaron Cicourel describes the dilemmas of a hypothetical new faculty member at a large university:

> He is faced with a number of status dilemmas because of the way his colleagues introduce themselves or the way he introduces himself to them. Do they (or he) use first names, last names, formal titles, or "Mr", or do they use their full name and refrain from calling him by his name. . . . The ways in which our young instructor "presents" himself will convey different connotations to different "others" depending on his physical appearance, clothing, language, and more importantly, how and when his occupational status is revealed, whether after or during the initial encounter. . . . In his new status as professor, therefore, our colleague must generate "adequate" performances commensurate with his position through a continued sequence of encounters and exchanges with others. . . . New acquaintances may accept and impute considerable importance to him, but he must somehow "carry it off", and often without any explicit "norms" or "rules" to go by. We obviously do not hand our new instruc-

tor a "script" outlining his "role" in detail. (Cicourel 1974: 16–17)

Cicourel goes on to show that such matters are further complicated by the problematic relevance of varied frames of social reference, or "the relevance of actual, changing scenes, orienting the actor to possible courses of action, the organization of behavioral displays and their reflective evaluation by the actor" (1974: 32). The point of importance for Cicourel is that ideas regarding which rights and duties are pertinent to a given individual change from situation to situation, and they are almost inevitably viewed differently by various persons participating in a given situation. For the present analysis, however, the pertinence of Cicourel's discussion is his pointing to the dialectical relation between conceptions of "status" and the skilled execution of social action, of what Cicourel calls "carry[ing] it off." Although his status may already have been established by his Ph.D. and his appointment to a university faculty, Cicourel's hypothetical professor must nevertheless continually bring off his status by successfully generating skilled interaction appropriate to his position.

In such a context, it is highly significant that a solo recital ritualizes skilled role behavior. The isolation of the soloist from the audience establishes the status of the performer far more unambiguously than the doctoral degree and the academic contract established the status of Cicourel's hypothetical college professor, and the recitalist is under much more pressure to bring off her or his status through successful performance. The recital not only ritually enacts the principle of separating the individual from the group, but it does this in terms of another central issue of the "cult of the individual," namely that of the crucial uncertainty of the performer's skill in social interaction. At one with the fact that a recital is a ritual in the "cult of the individual," then, is the fact that a formal solo recital is also a rite of social performance skill and "talent."

The rather widespread idea that industrialized society is impoverished in ritual action is a form of ethnocentrism, one that renders other, supposedly more sacralized and ritually oriented societies as exotic. It is simply not true that collective ritual has diminished in contemporary society; the most that might be said is that contemporary Western culture is mobilized around different forms of ritual and different characterizations of sacred experience.

The dialectical relationship between conceptions of sacred and secular in American culture is of course pertinent here. The predominance of a "secular" political process is generally understood not only as essential to the preservation of the variety of religious practise in this country, but at the same time as the moral safeguard of individual liberty. The sacred quality of individual liberties in American culture can surely be taken as self-evident, and while no less a scholar than Giddens may complain that "it is by no means clear what corresponds to the 'church' in relation to the 'sacred' beliefs of moral individualism" (Giddens 1977: 276), solo music recitals surely ritualize some of the most fundamental characteristics of those beliefs.

The cultural value of individualism is not an airborne concept that resides passive and inert in the minds of Europeans and Americans, nor is it simply an ideational by-product of a highly differentiated division of labor. Although the tie between individualism and the division of labor is important and unmistakable, the cultural value of individualism is also produced and reproduced through ritual action.

# Stage Fright and Tension

The emotion of stage fright is not only a central element in a performer's experience of the recital, it is also a key datum for the anthropological analysis of musical performance, since it melds social, emotional, and physiological experience. While the social and the physiological aspects of stage fright must of course both be understood, it must be remembered that these domains are distinct only in the analysis: for the performer, they are one, a congeries. The limitations of a purely sociological analysis can be seen in the comments of Clifford Geertz, who in the context of a discussion of the concept of self in Balinese culture describes the experience of stage fright with the rhetorical lilt that characterizes so much of his theorizing:

> Stage fright consists, of course, in the fear that, for want of skill or self-control, or perhaps by mere accident, an aesthetic illusion will not be maintained, that the actor will show through his part. Aesthetic distance collapses, the audience (and the actor) lose sight of Hamlet and gain it, uncomfortable for all concerned, of bumbling John Smith painfully miscast as the Prince of Denmark. (Geertz 1976: 230)

The tension generated by the separation of the actor from the part is too readily grasped when, as in Geertz's example, the first is named John Smith and the second is named Hamlet. The fact is that very much the same tension is manifested in situations where there is no comparable duality of personage. There are many cases in which there is a problem such as the one characterized by Sartre:

> Let us consider this waiter in the cafe. His movement is quick and forward, a little too precise, a little too rapid. He comes toward the patrons with a step a little too quick. He bends forward a little too eagerly; his voice, his eyes express an interest a little too solicitous for the order of the customer . . . his gestures and even his voice seem to be mechanisms; he gives himself the quickness and pitiless rapidity of things. He is playing, he is amusing himself. But what is he playing? We need not watch long before we can explain it: he is playing at being a waiter in a cafe. (Sartre, quoted in Laing 1961: 44)

Apart from the fact that Sartre's waiter seems to have spontaneously chosen to play at being a waiter, this account corresponds to many situations when a student is performing in a solo recital. In many if not most cases the student both *is* the recitalist and yet feels very foreign to the role and thus must also *play at being* a recitalist. This point is important to an understanding both of critical evaluations of performance by and among conservatory musicians, and of the self-presentation strategy of the performer.

Evaluative criticism in the conservatory hinges on the extent to which a performer is perceived as personally at one with her or his role. Geertz is at least partially wrong in suggesting that for the actor to show through the role is a matter of fear, the stuff of stage fright. A revealing of the person in the role is also a positive goal of artistic performance. To be sure, the bumblings of a John Smith will both impede the theatrical production and redound to his personal discredit. On the other hand, however, the eloquence of a Laurence Olivier will not only augment a production of *Hamlet*, but Olivier playing Hamlet (or Othello, Lear, or Shylock) has certainly brought personal and professional credit to Olivier himself. What constitutes failure is not that, but how, an actor shows through the part: what constitutes failure is the appearance of, for example, "John Smith painfully miscast." The fumbling fingers of a Jane Smith may both vulgarize a piano recital and confirm a negative perception of her, but the virtuosity of a Horowitz not only rewards the members of his audience but also redounds to the personal and artistic credit of Horowitz himself. Stage fright is not so much the fear that an "aesthetic illusion" will not be maintained, but more the fear that an aesthetic posture will manifest itself as an illusion, as a pose. Stage fright is not simply the fear that the person will show through the role, but that when the person does show through the role, it will reveal an incongruity of the person in that particular role.

The distinction between person and role is also, of course, of fundamental importance in the performer's strategy of self-presentation on stage. A clear example of a student who "was" the recitalist but who also was conscious of having to play at being the recitalist can be seen in the remarks made by a student who had recently played her conservatory Master's degree recital:

> God, it's scary to be out there, you're so ultra-conscious of everything, what your fingers are doing and everything, you know, a cough in the audience, anything. . . . It's hard to be yourself, so the more you can get comfortable in that atmosphere, obviously the better you are. . . . I wish I'd been trained as a performer ever since I was five, you know. I mean, that wouldn't have made me a very well-rounded person, but it makes you comfortable on stage. . . . Oh, yeah, you can put on a great facade . . . but inside [*laughs*], you know. . . . It's not like you're really even nervous, it's just that you think, oh am I going to get through this. . . . You're trying to get your thoughts on the music and making it speak, so it's hard, it's hard. But it was fun.

I had been in the audience at this student's recital, and had been struck by the fact that even though she did have some noticeable slip-ups in her performance, she maintained a very pleasant and self-assured appearance throughout her recital. The fact that she referred to her own assured appearance as a "facade" is indeed an indication of the self-conscious and strategic nature of her demeanor, and yet it would be both degrading to her and misleading for the analysis to suggest that what she called a facade is either superficial or fundamentally false. Deliberately maintaining a poised appearance, that is, maintaining the role of the solo performer, is an unquestionably important element in bringing off a performance. The performer who makes no attempt to maintain such a facade abdicates interest in the success of the event.

I once saw the famous mime Marcel Marceau perform a skit that dramatized the kind of problem faced by performing musicians. The skit depicted a mask maker trying on a variety of striking face masks, until suddenly the mask maker is unable to remove one of the masks, a *commedia del l'arte*–type smile. The mask maker grows increasingly desperate in his efforts to remove the mask, and is eventually reduced to heaving sobs of despair at his powerlessness to be rid of his smile. In this skit there is a person (Marceau) portraying a "person" (the mask maker) who is in turn portraying, through the device of wearing a mask, yet another "person" (the stock comic figure). The power of this performance is in the way it calls attention to the ability of one individual to manifest three distinct personages at the same time. The impact of this performance comes from the ability of Marceau to control the gestures and expressions of his body in a way that simultaneously represents two non-Marceau personages.

In similar fashion, the musician who feels nervous and uncomfortable in the role of solo performer must project an image that is quite at odds with her or his present emotional self experience. The nervous performer must, like the mime, maintain a facade. In exactly this sense, the student recitalist was maintaining a facade, but by the same token, it is significant that in retrospect, after describing her fears and the difficulties of maintaining her concentration during the performance, she concluded by saying, "it was fun." It is clear from her comments that she knew that additional experience in performing—and in maintaining a performer's facade—would eventually make everything easier. With additional performing experience, she will in all likelihood have fewer and smaller slip-ups and less and less difficulty maintaining her facade. An important part of the reason for this will be that over time she will no longer experience it *as* a facade; she will no longer feel a split between her role as solo performer and her personal identity in this role.

Although, from a sociological perspective the problem of stage fright is one of the tension between the person and the role, stage fright must also be understood as a problem of extremely refined motor control in the context of social and emotional tension. As already mentioned, these two aspects of the problem are distinguishable only in the abstraction of analysis. As our student soloist remarked in the preceding interview segment, a performer on stage is often simultaneously conscious of everything from minute finger movements to little coughs in the audience, and the fact is that from the facial muscles that generate a "forced" smile to the hand motions that generate a *pianissimo* trill on the concert stage, fine motor control is imperiled by personal stress. The importance of this fact for musical performance is of course due to the truly extraordinary amount of fine motor control, which musicians call "technique," requisite of anyone who would be a musical performer.

# The Limits of Technique and the Control of Anxiety

Probably the most basic requisite of anyone in the role of performer is a technical mastery of the musical instrument. To this end, long periods of practising or rehearsing, typically alone in a small practise studio, are the order of the conservatory student's day even in normal circumstances. Much—and in some cases, most—of this practising is done on exercises: scales, chords, or arpeggios designed explicitly for training the student in the physical mastery of the particular instrument or voice. Such work often takes on characteristics of body building: pianists work to increase the strength and speed of their fingers in order later to be able to play the difficult and strenuous passages of their repertoire, and violinists work for similarly long hours at, for example, eliminating any weakness or tremor in their bow arm so as to improve the tone quality of their playing. The "body-building" character of practising can also be seen in many instances in which musicians effectively treat the more difficult segments of their repertoire—a Beethoven sonata, say, or a Brahms concerto—as exercises, isolating brief passages for seemingly countless repetitions, until it can be played properly.

This kind of fine-toothed–comb practising, however, is by no means simply a matter of muscle building. From my own experience as a pianist preparing recital programs for performance, I remember the extent to which such repetitious treatment of short portions of repertoire also have a character of musical contemplation: an apt comparison would be a long, attentive gaze concentrating on a small detail of a masterful painting. A pianist (or any other kind of musician) is indeed training and developing muscular strength and coordination in this kind of rehearsing, but there is inevitably an important element of musical contemplation involved in this activity. For a pianist to train the fingers to a mastery, for example, of the trills of Beethoven's Sonata opus 109 is not only to discipline the muscles of the hand in a highly specific function, it is also to engage the pianist's body physically in a masterwork by a great composer. Such practising is a sensual kind of contemplation, a meditative muscle training.

There are, nevertheless, significant perils to such lengthy and intense rehearsing. The exaggerated attention that performing musicians give to such fine and minute details of muscular training can and occasionally does result in serious injury. During my stay at the conservatory, for example, there was a violin student who developed a very painful condition in his right hand while preparing for his Master's recital. Shortly after completing his recital, the pain became sufficiently great that he sought medical attention, and his doctor told him that real damage was being done to the muscles and nerves in his hand. Not surprisingly, he became quite concerned regarding the possible effect of this problem on the possibilities of his having a music career. His fears on this matter were grounded not only in his own pain and the doctor's admonition to curtail playing for two-week period, but also from his knowledge of the considerable problems of this sort encountered by violinists and other instrumentalists.

He told me that the problem was caused by a bad habit of pressing too much with the index finger of his bow hand, of overextending himself in effort to get a stronger sound from his violin. For him, the cure required not only therapeutic rest and relaxation, but also learning a different bow-arm technique. Nevertheless, although an improper technique is unquestionably liable to be a factor leading toward just this sort of physical injury, it cannot meaningfully be said that injuries to musical performers are caused only by faulty technique. One reason for saying this is simply that what is proper technique for one person may not be optimal for another person with different sized or shaped hands, arms, or vocal tract. The more general fact, however, is that the musician's almost unending quest for improved technique entails long hours of strenuous and taxing work, which tends to bring the risk of injury to even the most skilled of performers.

A celebrated example of this is the case of the eminent American pianist Leon Fleisher, whose career has been largely eclipsed for two decades due to a peculiar neural and muscular problem in his right hand, a problem clearly linked to his excessively arduous practising. A similar problem has plagued Gary Graffman, another prominent present-day pianist whose well-established concert career has been curtailed by a debilitating and painful neural problem in his hand. Of course, the semitragic role of the virtuoso performer whose career is ruined by such a maiming of the hand takes on heroic grandeur in the person of Robert Schumann, the great nineteenth-century composer who turned to composing only after ruining his career as a virtuoso pianist by irreparably injuring his hand in a mechanical contraption designed to enable him to increase the independence and strength of his right ring finger.

The prominence of Leon Fleisher and Gary Graffman does not in itself suffice to characterize extensive practising as a generally hazardous undertaking—clearly most concert artists are able to follow a performing career without encountering such unfortunate difficulties. Nevertheless, the cases of Fleisher and Graffman are at least representative of the hazards of excessive practising on a musical instrument.

Singers in the conservatory, for example, were on constant guard against such vocalizing as might injure their vocal chords, and although I encountered only one consequential practise-related injury during my stay at the conservatory (that of the violin student already mentioned), I had encountered performers with numerous injuries of varying degrees of seriousness during my earlier career as a performing musician. Such problems are not endemic, but neither are they extraordinary. They illustrate the fact that the importance of mastering musical performance skills is such that musicians sometimes dangerously, indeed destructively, go beyond the physiological limits of their own body. These injuries are indices of the intensity of these people's commitment. In connection with the discussion of the contemplative nature of such practising, the word "devotion" would also be appropriate to their roles as musical performers.

It should be readily understood that the avoidance of excessive physical tension is an important concern in the teaching and learning of musical performance skills. Controlled relaxation is a central element in some musicians' very conception of technique, and as such is for many performers a matter for ongoing attention in the course of instrumental study. Also, however, the issue of physical and psychological tension is sometimes treated at some length as a distinct and separate problem, as it was in a lecture/seminar in the conservatory by Dorothea Budryk, a visiting specialist on the avoidance of tension in piano performance.

"I approach the problem from two angles," she said, "inner nervous tension and muscular tension. The nervous tension is harder to deal with, but the fact is that nervous and muscular tension are not isolated, but rather, come together." She viewed the pianist's body as in effect the repository of the social and emotional tensions of the performance situation. As she coached individual students on proper posture at the piano, she said, "I want the whole body to disappear." This, or course, meant only that controlled relaxation of the body was the optimal way to eliminate the tensions of performance nervousness. What she really wanted to disappear were the fear-related tensions of the body.

Although oriented toward problems very different from those encountered in Marcus Goldmann's chamber music class, like him Budryk focused on the importance of breathing. She pointed out that inhaling tends to be tension producing and conversely that exhaling tends toward relaxation. In a moment of anxiety or startlement, she noted, a person has a tendency to gasp, to inhale and then hold the breath; this tendency, she emphasized, must be overcome. "There is probably no such thing as a performance without nervousness," she said, but at the same time, "there is only one antidote to nervousness, and that's exhalation. Everything the pianist wants, happens during exhalation—the shoulders drop, the neck relaxes, and the hands become warmer." She pointed out four principle centers of physical tension for the pianist: the back of the neck, the shoulders, the wrists, and the face. She insisted that it is incumbent upon the pianist to be certain that these four areas were kept in a properly relaxed, or, as she repeatedly put it, "balanced" state. "Anxiety doesn't live happily in a body which is in a state of balance."

Indeed, a primary point to be taken from her presentation is the extent to which physical relaxation was presented as a means, a technique, of controlling emotional tensions. Her sentence "anxiety doesn't live happily in a body which is in a state of balance" is not only curious in its incongruous anthropomorphism (I, at least, am confused by the image of "anxiety" *living* "happily"), but is also important for its implicit notion of personal agency. Stated negatively, what is significant is that she did not say the converse, that an anxious person will not be able to keep the body in a state of balance. Her point here was that the way to contend with performance anxiety is through physical relaxation, that anxiety and emotional tension could and must be managed through controlled relaxation of the body.

Thus in spite of her opening comment that she approached the problem of tension in terms of two aspects, physical and psychological, the preponderance of her presentation was oriented toward the physical relaxation of the performer's body. In contrast—and yet at the same time, in close association—with the fact that a performer's "technique" entails the extreme development of the various kinds of fine motor control already discussed, a major point of Budryk's presentation was that since the social and emotional tensions of stage fright are also manifested physically in the performer's body, controlled physical relaxation can for the performer be a "technique" for dealing with the emotional tensions engendered in the performance situation. The tensions of stage fright are manifested simultaneously as social, emotional, and bodily/muscular tensions; a musician's "technique" must in the broadest sense be understood as including bodily control of the performance situation as well as of the instrument.

# "Chops, but No Soul"

In her presentation Budryk made brief mention of the recent development of a drug that combats the effects of stage fright by chemically diminishing the body's production of adrenaline. She referred to an experiment in which several musical performers were administered the drug while others were given a placebo, with the results clearly indicating improved performance in connection with the drug. Nevertheless, Budryk expressed her opposition to such practises: "I'm antidrug," she said. "One simply doesn't know the side effects of this sort of thing."

I did not ask the other people in the conservatory how they felt about the issue of taking a drug to alleviate stage fright, but I would infer at least the possibility of a more specifically esthetic reason for being opposed to the use of drugs for such purposes. My reason for saying this comes from comments made to me in interviews with conservatory students who evaluated for me their own and other students' recital performances. The issues raised in these interviews ranged across a broad spectrum of concerns, but uppermost among them was the idea that in a formal recital the true, inner person must indeed show through the role of the highly skilled performing artist. To me, at least, this seems implicitly incompatible with the idea of a soloist performing while under the influence of a drug.

The distinction between the mechanical, technical mastery of performance techniques and the emotional, personal, interpretive expression of a performer is, I would argue, the single most fundamental esthetic issue for conservatory musicians. Just as a performer must, as was discussed in the previous chapter, play what the text indicates but not play something simply because the text so indicates, a performer must also play with technical control of the repertoire and yet not manifest a simply technical mastery of the music. These two principles are closely related: they are, one might say, both analogous and homologous. In both contexts the issue is that of playing with feeling, and in both cases the determination of this is interpretive and subjective. A conservatory washroom graffito put the matter succinctly: "chops, but no soul."

These originally Afro-American terms appear to have been adapted into conservatory lingo since I was a music student in the early 1960s, and have gained widespread usage as synonyms, respectively, of technique and musicality. These concepts constitute the distinction between the mechanical and the expressive aspects of musical performance. The chops/soul and technique/musicality concepts are dualistic in nature, and are meaningful mainly as contrasted with each other. Moreover, they are frequently spoken with an unmistakably moral import. While technique is seen as essential to adequate musical performance, sheer technique is disdained almost as though it were a form of carnal knowledge. Sheer technique is as distinct from truly musical performance as sheer sex might be from true love.

Although distinctions between chops and soul, or between technique and musicality, are indeed highly subjective and inferential, their sociological implication is clear and unambiguous: they are conceptualizations for distinguishing the one from the many, for postulating the uniqueness of an individual performer as distinct from the more standardized collectivity. In the words of one conservatory student whom I had asked to comment on the chops but no soul expression: "Some people are always looking to say that people who have technique really aren't musical, but that just leads to the issue of competition." The contrasts between chops and soul or between technique and musicality do not themselves provide any objective criterion for distinguishing the uniquely artistic individual from the average conservatory student. The meanings of these terms are highly contingent and variable, and they clearly have no power or agency of their own.

The mechanical-technical/emotional-expressive dualism entails implicit notions of the nature of the performer as an individual, or more specifically, notions regarding the moral worth of the inner person as contrasted with the performance skills of the trained musician. The cult of the individual is strongly in evidence in this important esthetic principle, and the spiritualist connotation of the word *soul* is highly significant. Perhaps especially since the term derives from Afro-American culture, it must be made clear that the meaning of the term as used in the conservatory differs in at least one important respect from that of urban black culture as described by Charles Keil (1966: 164–190). The musician with "soul" in Afro-American parlance is one who embodies the collective experience of black American subculture, whereas by contrast the musician who performs with "soul" in the conservatory thereby is distinguished from the others; such a musician is seen to embody, one might say, the highest qualities of "everyman" by manifesting an inner uniqueness.

One of the notions used most commonly by musicians to characterize the relationship between sheer technique and truly expressive playing is that of the willingness to take risks. Of course, the very act of walking out on stage constitutes a risk in itself—such is the essential nature of stage fright, of singing "the Lord's song in a strange land."

However, when musicians in the conservatory talk about taking risks, they are referring to a far more subjective experience than a decision not to remain forever backstage. The risk in question is that of exposing imperfections in one's technique, in one's performance skill or training. The risk is that of possibly playing some wrong notes, or playing with a scratchy violin tone, or singing with a poorly modulated voice. To return to the sociological formulation of Geertz, the risk is that of exposing the soloist as miscast—inadequately prepared, trained, or disciplined—in the performer's role.

At the same time, the soloist must not convey an impression of overcautiously rehearsing in public, or of playing in a way that displays only highly trained control of the instrument. The importance of this side of the equation lies in the fact that in the conservatory there is an implicit presumption of a considerable amount of technique, and that what is at issue among conservatory musicians is a performer's willingness to try to transcend this technique, to put the technical performing skill into the service of expressing the composer's intentions. An important aspect of the very notion of "music" is entailed here as well: in conservatory parlance, a performer must be willing to take risks in order to be musical, or in order to play the music, rather than just the notes.

The following comments by a conservatory violinist illustrate the value that musicians put on taking risks in the interests of really producing the music. These remarks indicate the close connection between the sacralized conception of an artistic individual and a morally charged conception of music—conceptions that occupy a central place in conservatory values. The comments came in the middle of an interview in which the violinist was giving a phrase-by-phrase evaluation of a taped performance of Schoenberg's *Verklärte Nacht*. The point he is making concerns the fact that as a violinist approaches the end of a "down-bow," the tone quality of the violin is likely to deteriorate unless the violinist "changes bows," that is, reverses the direction of the bow's motion. A long, slow down-bow entails the danger of a scratchy tone at the end: the risk, in this case, is that of sustaining the long down-bow—and of producing a poor tone—in order to give the "musically" proper rhythmic thrust to the phrase.

VIOLINIST: I'll show you where the second violinist—where it goes Daaa daa-ee da da deee . . . and, you know, it's a dotted quarter note and an eighth note, the second violin, because you go teeem, taa . . . tee. You have to move the bow back, in one eighth note, whereas you've had three. It's easy to change early, tee, taa-dee, which is just a sloppy bad habit of not really thinking about the music, because it's technically easy to do, you know. . . . And I said to her, a whole bunch of times, you know, one, two, daa-deeeee, you know, she never got it, she wasn't—

HK: Now, let me make sure I've got this right. It's a long down-bow, and then you have to get—

VIOLINIST: It's Daa DEEEEE Daaa da Deeeeeee, Daa DEEEEE—you see, so you have to do a very fast up-bow . . . if you're playing in time. And it's easy to go, Daaaaaaa DEEE Daaa da Daaaa-Daaaaaa DEEE, you know—

HK: Start a little too early?

VIOLINIST: Yeah, to start early. . . . Maybe she wanted to stretch it, but I think it, you know, she wanted to deee deee, daaa daaa deee, but if you're going to stretch it, you should stretch it at the end of the line, not in the measure before, you know what I mean?

HK: What you're saying is that she was probably—

VIOLINIST: She was more concerned about—

HK: She was trying to make more sure that she got to that note at the top.

VIOLINIST: Well, she was more concerned about her violin tone than about producing the music, at that point, you see? And to me it'd be much more important to go deeee, da DEEE, and maybe you'd have to struggle a bit, to really produce a good sound on that long note, 'cause you have to hold it, but, but it creates, you know, a musical effect. . . . Maybe it's not the best example, but that's the kind of thing that I mean. That's why I'm interested in going for it, in taking a risk, almost to the last minute: deeee, DAAA Dee—To me that's what the music's indicating, and that's more important to me than tone.

# "Serious" Music and Individualism

There are almost certainly no musicians in the conservatory who would characterize a Mozart sonata or a Beethoven string quartet as "sacred" music. Conservatory music is of course "secular" in the everyday Western sense that it belongs to a domain quite distinct from churches and Sabbaths. To me, however, the latter seems an unduly restricted and ethnocentric categorization for use in anthropological analysis. There is a different sense in which conservatory music deserves to be considered as "sacred."

Music is, among other things, an idiom of collective emotional experience, experience that is expressed and renewed in ritual action. In the conservatory, formal recitals provide a clear example of just such ritual action. The analytic benefit of treating recitals as rituals has been to clarify the connection between musical performance and some central notions of contemporary American culture, primarily, in this case, those of moral individualism.

The notion of "serious music," a phrase that is widely used to designate Western art music, provides an insight to the "sacred" character of this musical idiom. It should be self evident that the word *serious* in the phrase *serious music* is not to be taken as contrasted with, say, funny, frivolous, or silly. If anything, it is understood as a contrast to "popular" music, or perhaps to folk music, rock, or jazz. When folksinger Pete Seeger sings "The Bells of Rhymney," whose words are grim indeed, he is not performing serious music in the sense usually given that phrase. Nor was jazzman Freddie Hubbard, when he recorded the album *Sing me a Song of Songmy*. In the phrase *serious music*, the word *serious* doesn't just mean serious—it means something much more like "sacred." Of course, it is not an equivalent term, for while it may be significant to note the Biblical texts of Brahm's "Four Serious Songs" (*Vier ernste Gesänge*), musicians do acknowledge a specific category of sacred music, consisting primarily of Christian liturgical chants, motets, choral masses, and the like. The phrase *serious music* sits squarely on the boundary between the sacred and secular domains. Serious music is both sacred and secular. More precisely, it beggars the distinction.

The analysis of solo recitals as rituals has led to the realization that there are contexts in which the very concept of music can be used to characterize an individual as distinguished from the group, or perhaps more specifically, to distinguish an extraordinary performer from a more ordinary one. Such an association of serious music with individualism is closely linked to the notion of taking risks. In order to sing a song in a strange land, one must be willing to take risks. For the Old Testament Israelites the risk would have been that of ridicule—or worse—at the hands of the Babylonians; the rhetoric of the psalm suggests that such a risk may not have been taken. For the conservatory student the risk is that of being perceived as miscast in the role, of being exposed as an inadequately skilled performer. The conservatory student, however, must take this risk, or be characterized as one who only plays the notes, that is, as one who is not musical. This individual must be willing to risk technical chops in the interest of musical soul.

# SIX

# A CULTURAL SYSTEM

## Concepts of Music

As I began my research at the Eastern Metropolitan Conservatory, my intent was to study terms of evaluation. My plan was to examine the concepts and criteria used in evaluating music and musicians by students and teachers in the conservatory. Such a plan entailed an underlying dualism, one derived in part from Edmund Leach's formulation (discussed in Chapter One) regarding the relation between ethics and esthetics, that is, between social action on the one hand and cultural form on the other. My "hypothesis," if it may be called such, was that negotiations of social identity and evaluations of music would be reciprocally effecting—that many esthetic evaluations of musical performance would entail implicit ethical evaluations of the persons performing (e.g., "her Mozart lacked feeling"), and conversely that ethical evaluations of people would embody underlying esthetic statements about musical performance (e.g., "she doesn't have any talent").

A second, and more sharply drawn, dualism in my original research plan derived from my training in ethnomusicology, a field that has for many years been contending with Alan P. Merriam's early argument that "the dual nature of ethonomusicology is clearly a fact of the discipline" (Merriam 1964: 17). There is arguably no idea more entrenched and pervasive in the field of ethnomusicology than that of the dualism between the study of music and the study of culture, unless one counts separately the corollary notion that the goal of theory in ethnomusicology is precisely to bridge the gap that separates these two domains. "Such a fusion is clearly the objective of ethnomusicology and the keystone upon which the validity of its contribution lies" (Merriam 1964: 17). This dualism has presented itself as a pressing, even troubling, dilemma for many ethnomusicologists. Although in 1982 the editor of *Ethnomusicology* announced that "we seem to be on the verge of overcoming the split between musicological and anthropological approaches that characterized the first twenty-five years [of the Society for Ethnomusicology]" his comment appears to have been based at least partly on hope. "With some luck and determination, ethnomusicology will 'come of age' . . . as a discipline with a unique perspective that fuses these two approaches" (Rice 1982: v). A short while earlier, however, David McAllester had articulated the view of many ethnomusicologists: "musicology and anthropology have proven to be uneasy bedfellows" (McAllester 1980: 305).

In view of these two dualisms, and perhaps more significantly in view of the fact that my research plan was oriented toward the concepts and terms that were at issue in evaluating conservatory music and musicians, it is significant that one of the first "findings" of my conservatory research was that no term is used more consistently as a concept of evaluation than the word *music* itself. For example, orchestra conductor Tom Vosniak would stop the orchestra in rehearsal with the complaint, "Oohh, come on, you should be *making music* together!" Similarly Andy Marelli, in the midst of a session of *solfege* exercises, told the students in his sight-singing class that "you must never think of these as *music*—these are *drills*." (It will be recalled that a similar remark of his, to the effect that conservatory students of recent years have declined "musically," even while showing increased skills in performance technique and music literacy, was discussed in Chapter One.) The comment quoted in Chapter Five, regarding the second violinist who was "more concerned about her violin tone than about producing the music," provides another representative example.

In other words, conservatory evaluations were less often a matter of whether the music was in some way good or bad than a matter of whether what someone had done was really "music." Rather than an objective domain that was itself evaluated and judged, the concept of music seemed to be a first and most central notion used in making value judgments. The archetypal example of this came on one of my first visits to Marcus Goldmann's chamber music class. Here I listened with the score (often referred to as "the music") on my lap to two young students playing a portion of a Beethoven duo sonata, only to hear Mr. Goldmann chide the pianist because she wasn't playing the music, she was only playing "the notes."

I occasionally discussed this shifting character of the music category with the conservatory musicians. Their response to my observation was frequently one of mildly amused curiosity, but they often had observations of their own to make on the matter. In the context of a chat with a trumpet student who, as it happened, was standing in a hallway waiting for his weekly lesson, I mentioned that I had been struck by and was thinking about the different senses of the word *music*, and in particular with the notion of playing the music as contrasted with playing the notes. He responded by saying that Mr. Pepicelli, one of the orchestra conductors, was very good at getting students to really play the music, and that what was really interesting was that he did this by talking about things that were nonmusical. He said that, for example, Mr. Pepicelli would tell the orchestra members that when he made a cue with the baton, the orchestra players should try to imagine the cue as having been thrown, like a ball, and that they should respond like the ball caroming off the wall. What this trumpet student had put his finger on was the fact that a verbal image (in other contexts categorically nonmusical or "extramusical") was frequently at the very core of "the actual music," that is to say, of playing musically, or with feeling (this, of course, is largely the same point as was made above in Chapter Four in the context of Marcus Goldmann's teaching).

The variable nature of the music concept was not associated

exclusively with evaluative judgments on particular performers and performances. It sometimes referred fairly simply to what can only be called a conservatory division of labor. At least partially within this category would be Andy Marelli's remark regarding the distinction between music and the drills that made up the basis of the sight-singing and ear-training class. A still clearer instance of this came in the conservatory's "diction for singers" class, which was in a particular but generally understood sense a class dealing with nonmusical issues. The teacher would frequently parry questions with comments on the order of "that's a musical question, we don't deal with those problems in this class," and students, knowing this, would occasionally hedge their questions by saying, "I know this is a musical question, but . . ." At issue was whether or not the discussion was focused specifically on the proper enunciation of linguistic phonemes, those German vowels and Italian consonants that are so crucial in the singing of "classical" music's vocal repertoires. It should perhaps be specified that this was not a class in language, or even in "diction" in its primary sense denoting word usage; grammatical syntax was never at issue here, and although much lip service was paid to the idea that singers must always know the meanings of the words they are singing, it was frequently apparent that they did not. This was a class which dealt with skills specific to musical performance, thus contrasting it quite directly with the sight-singing class. Nevertheless, each was in its own way conceived as nonmusic.

This fluctuating nature of the music concept raises problems for a dualistic music-and-culture (or esthetics-and-ethics) approach. The relation between music and cultural context becomes as slippery as quicksilver when we realize that what is taken to be music changes with context, not to mention the fact that reference to any context can entail an almost indefinite regress of intercontextuality. The notion of music is comparable with the notion of the sacred as discussed in the previous chapter: just as a notion of the sacred is contrasted not only with the profane but also with other notions of the sacred, any particular conception of music should be understood as set off not only from culture—or from nonmusic—but also from other senses of the word *music.*

The shifting character of the music notion relates to an observation made some sixty years ago by the pioneering anthropologist Edward Sapir:

> There are certain terms that have a peculiar property. Ostensibly, they mark off specific concepts, concepts that lay claim to a rigorously objective validity. In practise, they label vague terrains of thought that shift or narrow or widen with the point of view of whoso makes use of them, embracing within their gamut of significances conceptions that not only do not harmonize but are in part contradictory. (Sapir 1949: 308)

Clearly music is lacking what Sapir called "a rigorously objective validity." The music that is "conserved" in a conservatory of music is not a found object. An anthropologist does not arrive at the conservatory to find music an apparent and ready-made object of study, in the way that, for example, an archaeologist arrives at an excavation site to find (or perhaps fail to find) projectile points, potsherds, or prehistoric skeletal remains. In the conservatory, what was music to one person could be "the notes" to another, and "her violin tone" to yet another, while in other contexts all might agree that one should do what "the music," that is, the score, says to do. All of this notwithstanding, conservatory musicians continually referred to "the music" as though it were a constant, concrete, and unambiguous point of reference, a cultural *terra firma* of their social world.

Sapir provided what was at least the beginning of an explanation:

> An analysis of such terms soon discloses the fact that underneath the clash of varying contents there is unifying feeling-tone. What makes it possible for so discordant an array of conceptions

to answer to the same call is, indeed, precisely this relatively constant halo that surrounds them. Thus, what is "crime" to one man is "nobility" to another, yet both are agreed that crime, whatever it is, is an undesirable category, that nobility, whatever it is, is an estimable one. . . . We disagree on the value of things and the relations of things, but often enough we agree on the particular value of a label. It is only when the question arises of just where to put the label, that trouble begins. (1949: 308)

Sapir concluded his comments with reference to the variety of "pretenders" to such labels, arguing that "the rival pretenders war to the death; the thrones to which they aspire remain serenely splendid in gold."

This latter observation, at least, appears not to be applicable to the concept of music. Continuing with his anthropomorphic style of presentation, the various senses of the term "music" are not so much warring pretenders to a golden throne as they are interdependent workers on a common undertaking, or perhaps various players on a team. They are indeed different and contrasting, but they are interdependent as well.

Music is a cultural polymorph, rather like talent. It will be recalled that in Chapter Three I called attention to the polymorphic nature of talent, that is, to the fact that talent is manifested in countless ways—in music, sports, scholarship, flower arranging, and so forth—and to the fact that these various manifestations of talent are understood less as internally contradictory than as reciprocally confirming the validity and reality of each other. Thus we don't tend to say that since talent manifests itself in violin playing, singing, flower arranging, and basketball playing then talent really isn't real, but only a series of contradictions; we tend, rather, to say that these many manifestations of talent attest to the pervasive nature of the phenomenon. A comparable dynamic can be seen at work with the concept of "music": the many senses of the word have strikingly different meanings, and yet this variety of meaning clearly doesn't work in reciprocally self-contradicting ways (the fact that there are so many divergent senses of the word is not taken to show that there is really no such thing as music), but rather works as an interconnected cultural system. Rather than being mutually exclusive, these divergent senses of the word *music* are mutually dependent. This polymorphic nature of music is an important element in what I am calling a cultural system.

# Concepts of Culture

Although Sapir's comments were quoted in connection with the notion of music, the fact is that Sapir in making them was concerned not with music but with the concept of *culture*, with "advanc[ing] the claims of a pretender to the throne called 'culture'" (Sapir 1949: 308). The concept of "culture," of course, is itself open to any number of uses and interpretations, and among anthropologists the term has for some time shared a trait with borrowed money: we will use it, and even become dependent on it, although often we do not quite know how we will account for it.

Sapir's "pretender" to the notion of "culture" was a notion encompassing "civilization in so far as it embodies the national genius" (Sapir 1949: 311). Sapir proffered this conceptualization as a combining of two prior notions, one pertaining to individual refinement (e.g., characteristic of the "cultured" person who can recite Shakespeare and discuss Renaissance art), the other being what Sapir called the ethnologist's notion of culture. This would have been the notion articulated in the then-famous definition of Tylor: "Culture or Civilization, taken in its wide ethnographic sense, is that complex whole which includes knowledge, belief, art, morals, law, custom, and any other capabilities and habits acquired by man as a member of society" (Tylor 1958 [1871]: 1).

The conception of culture connoting "national genius" was associated with a school of anthropological thought known as the "culture and personality" school, in which different cultures, like different personalities, were said to be characterized by a configuration of salient traits and practises. For example, in the highly influential *Patterns of Culture* (1951) by Sapir's anthropological colleague Ruth Benedict, the Pueblos of the American southwest were classified as "Apollonian," most other native American cultures as "Dionysian." Significantly, Benedict's study was undertaken with a particular reflexive purpose: although present-day Western culture is altogether too complex for this kind of cultural analysis, "the facts of simpler cultures may make clear social facts [regarding Western culture] that are otherwise baffling and not open to demonstration. This is nowhere more true than in the matter of the fundamental and distinctive cultural configurations that pattern existence and condition the thoughts and emotions of the individuals who participate in those cultures" (Benedict 1951: 50). However, Benedict herself realized that many of even these "simple" societies are of sufficient complexity as to show a marked absence of cultural integration, and have no "characteristic psychological response that appear[s] to have arisen to dominate the culture as a whole" (1951: 207). Moreover, subsequent anthropological research made significant compromises regarding the validity of the generalized psychological characterizations of even those groups for whom such characterizations had seemed appropriate.

This is not the place, nor am I the person, for even a summary review of anthropological theories of culture. However, the widespread uncertainty regarding whether culture was a Benedictian organic configuration, a Tylorean "complex whole," or, in the phrase of Robert Lowie, a discontinuous "thing of shreds and patches" (Lowie 1961: 441), does provide a backdrop for the anthropological writing of Clifford Geertz, whose approach to the culture concept is of unquestionable importance to this study.

In 1966, Geertz remarked that "the term 'culture' has by now acquired a certain aura of ill-repute in social anthropological circles because of the multiplicity of its referents and the studied vagueness with which it has all too often been invoked" (Geertz 1973: 89). For this reason, an important thrust of Geertz's writings has been devoted to a "cutting of the culture concept down to size" (Geertz 1973: 4) through a focus on symbols and signification. "Believing, with Max Weber, that man is an animal suspended in webs of significance he himself has spun, I take culture to be those webs" (1973: 5). Thus for Geertz culture is "an historically transmitted pattern of meanings embodied in symbols, a system of inherited conceptions expressed in symbolic forms" (1973: 89). In turn, the study of culture concerns itself with "turning the analytic powers of semiotic theory . . . away from an investigation of signs in abstraction toward an investigation of them in their natural habitat—the common world in which men look, name, listen, and make" (1983: 119). This is one feature of anthropological inquiry that I have tried to bring to the study of music.

Among many present-day anthropologists the phrase "as a cultural system" is linked securely to Geertz's name, in part, although only in part, because he has published influential essays entitled "Religion as a Cultural System," "Ideology as a Cultural System," "Common Sense as a Cultural System," and "Art as a Cultural System" (Geertz 1973: 87–125, 193–233; 1983: 731–93, 94–120). In these essays Geertz argues that although religion, ideology, common sense, and art do indeed consist of sets of meaningful symbols, these systems are not formal unities made up of nicely integrated parts. Rather, they are inextricably intertwined with a variety of other cultural domains. Indeed, Geertz associates the shortcomings of earlier analyses of ideology with "the handling of ideology as an entity in itself—as an ordered system of cultural symbols rather than in the discrimination of its social and psychological contexts" (1973: 196).

In a similar vein, and one more immediately related to the present study, Geertz suggested that "it is perhaps only in the modern age and in the West that some people . . . have managed to convince themselves that technical talk about art, however developed, is sufficient to a complete understanding of it; that the whole secret of aesthetic power is located in the formal relations among sounds, images, volumes, themes, or gestures" (1983: 96). For Geertz the study of culture is the study of the ways in which various domains of meaning are associated and differentiated; the congruence between such an orientation and the present book's focus on the contexts and contextualization of music should be readily apparent.

One of Geertz's characterizations of anthropological interpretation is that of "rendering mere occurrences scientifically eloquent" (1973: 28), and he associates progress in anthropology with "refinement of debate. What gets better is the precision with which we vex each other" (1973: 29). In a spirit, then, of "vexed" homage I would apply Geertz's just-noted remark, regarding the importance of studying cultural symbols not in the abstract but in the environment of ongoing social activities, to another Geertz passage, this one dealing with music. Geertz proposes that if we

take, say, a Beethoven quartet as an, admittedly rather special but, for these purposes, nicely illustrative, sample of culture, no one would, I think, identify it with its score, with the skills and knowledge needed to play it, with the understanding of it possessed by its performers or auditors, nor, to take care, *en passant*, of the reductionists and reifiers, with a particular performance of it or with some mysterious entity transcending material existence. The "no one" is perhaps too strong here, for there are always incorrigibles. But that a Beethoven quartet is a temporally developed tonal structure, a coherent sequence of modeled sound—in a word, music—and not anybody's knowledge of or belief about anything, including how to play it, is a proposition to which most people are, upon reflection, likely to assent. (1973: 11–12)

The context of Geertz's comments on the Beethoven quartet is a critique of a school of thought known as "cognitive anthropology," and I will say that I share with Geertz his reservations regarding the idea that "culture" can be equated with "whatever it is one has to know or believe in order to operate in a manner acceptable to its members" (Goodenough, quoted in Geertz 1973: 11). Moreover, as Geertz notes, it is indeed fallacious to identify a Beethoven quartet with its score, with one or all performances of it, or with the performers' or listeners' understanding of it. But to say that a Beethoven quartet is "a temporally developed tonal structure," or "a coherent sequence of modeled sound," is to beg the question. And nothing of substance is added by identifying all of this with, "in a word, music." One need not be identifying a Beethoven quartet with its score in order to assert the fundamental and essential importance of the score to the quartet; the same can be said regarding this or that performance, these or those performers' skills, and the understanding of the audience. Indeed, to stress the crucial importance of each and all of these elements, working in an intercontextual system, seems to me a most appropriate way of characterizing a Beethoven quartet.

This, however, is only the beginning of it. Since Geertz suggests a Beethoven quartet, let us consider the Beethoven Quartet in B-flat Major, opus 130. This quartet has, in effect, two different final movements. The movement originally composed by Beethoven as the finale of this quartet was judged too long and difficult by various of Beethoven's contemporaries, and Beethoven, that exemplar of artistic rebellion and individualism, was prevailed upon by his publisher to compose a much smaller and accessible movement to replace it. The original finale, the *Grosse Fuge*, was published separately as opus 133, and musicologist Philip Radcliffe, for one, holds that this is as it should be.

The immensely varied moods expressed in the different sections of the Fugue [the *Grosse Fuge*] are best appreciated if it is regarded, not as the Finale of an already very extended work, but as a separate composition of symphonic dimensions containing within itself the contrasts usually associated with the familiar three- or four-movement scheme. (Radcliffe 1968: 137)

Musicologist Harold Truscott, among others, disagrees: "that the fugue remained the proper finale to the work there is no doubt, and today there are far more performances with the fugue than with the alternative finale . . . that it is essentially a quartet movement, albeit a very difficult one, is certainly true" (Truscott 1968: 133). Which, then, is to be considered the true, or the appropriate, closing movement of this quartet? One can be confident that this question will live forever.

I must, of course, confess to a certain malice aforethought in selecting opus 130; the problem of choosing from among multiple movements does not pertain to the other Beethoven string quartets. And yet, if any Beethoven quartet provides an appropriate analogue to the notion of "culture," it is opus 130, for it is this quartet that best illustrates the truth that cultural forms inevitably engender social negotiations, interaction characterized by uncertainty and contention, as well as continual and highly contingent evaluations of coherence and incoherence. "Coherence," "sequence," and "modeling," to use Geertz's concepts, are problematic and at issue, and this not only in Beethoven's opus 130, not only in music, but also, as Geertz clearly knows, in "culture" generally.

An anthropological notion of "culture," then, is both manifested and unraveled (or, as literary theorists might say, "deconstructed") within Geertz's essays. The adjective *cultural* and the phrase *cultural system* are in these writings unquestionably more felicitous than the simple noun, *culture*. Geertz's claim that "culture is public because meaning is" (Geertz 1973: 12) entails an assumption that "culture" is a domain both interdependent upon and, in real life, inextricable from another domain, private experience, yet conceived theoretically as foreign to it. The antagonistic interdependence of the "cult of the individual" and the "cult of John Doe," discussed in the previous chapter, provided a case study of this problem.[1]

In such a context it is significant that some anthropologists (e.g., Ortner 1984, Yengoyan 1986) have noted a general movement away from the "culture" concept in current anthropological theory. Others (Marcus 1980, Marcus and Cushman 1982, Marcus and Fischer 1986) have argued that the point of central concern for anthropology lies not in the reality of "culture," or of what actually goes on while the anthropologist does "fieldwork," but rather in writing, in the anthropological/ethnographic text. Marcus, for example, argues that the

> fundamental question . . . is the characteristic manner by which a text's language and organization convinces its readers of the truth, or at least the credibility, of its claims. . . . Anthropology's development of knowledge has proceeded more by changes in its rhetoric than by close conformity to a rhetoric-denying scientific model, concerned with rules of evidence and verification. (Marcus 1980: 508)

Marcus points to the increasing willingness of scholars to weave references to their personal dilemmas of interpreting fieldwork into anthropological texts as one of the most significant developments in present-day anthropological writing. In this connection, while I have not tried in this book to write what Marcus might categorize as a "confessional" account, I would emphasize once again that my conception of a cultural system is not intended as one drawing solely on the terminology of anthropological theory, but rather as one also grounded in my own experience. Just as Geertz suggested that "theoretical formulations hover so low over the interpretations they govern that they don't make much sense or hold much interest apart from them" (Geertz 1973: 25), I would argue that cultural interpretations embody so clearly the perspective of their authors that pretensions in them of scientific objectivity can only diminish their credibility.

# Meaning and Social Order

Of course, Geertz is neither the first nor the only anthropologist to focus on problems of cultural meaning. There is a long and distinguished tradition that focuses on the sociological implications of variety and disjunction in the meanings of important cultural concepts. Prominent in this tradition is *Nuer Religion*, in which E. E. Evans-Pritchard deals at considerable length with the myriad and contrasting senses of the Nuer word *kwoth*. Evans-Pritchard begins his study with the announcement that "the Nuer word we translate 'God' is *kwoth*, Spirit" (1956: 1). However, the central theme of Evans-Pritchard's discussion is that although the representation of a pervasive and immaterial being is the most basic and fundamental meaning of *kwoth*, the same word is used by Nuer in strikingly different, indeed seemingly contradictory, senses. Besides *kwoth* translated as "God" or "Spirit," Evans-Pritchard notes "that there are besides divers particular spirits each of which is also *kwoth* and that the word has a plural form, *kuth*, by which are indicated a number of such spirits" (1956: 28).

Evans-Pritchard's presentation is a complex discussion of unity in diversity, of the whole in the parts, of the one in the many: "spirits of the air are conceived of as both separate beings and yet also as different manifestations of God" (1956: 48). Similarly, "rain and pestilence come from God and are therefore manifestations of him, and in this sense rain and pestilence are God, in the sense that he reveals himself in their falling. But though one can say of rain or pestilence that it is God one cannot say of God that he is rain or pestilence" (1956: 125). A central point in Evans-Pritchard's analysis is that an anthropological interpretation of such a concept requires an understanding of the social organization in connection with which the concept is used:

> The conclusion we have reached is that the conception of *kwoth*
> has a structural dimension. At one end Spirit is thought of in

relation to man and the world in general as omnipresent God. Then it is thought of in relation to a variety of social groups and activities and to categories of persons: to political movements connected with prophets, and in a special relation to warfare, as spirits of the air; to descent groups as *colwic* and totemic spirits; and to a variety of ritual specialists as totemic, totemistic, and similar spirits. At the other end, it is conceived of more or less in relation to individuals in a private capacity as nature sprites and fetishes. God figured as common father and creator is patron of political leaders; figured in *colwic* and totemic spirits, and also in unnamed refractions, he is patron of lineages and families; and figured in nature sprites and fetishes he is patron of individuals. (1956: 117)

A reader of Evans-Pritchard's account (perhaps especially a reader more concerned with Western "classical" music than with African religions!) may be inclined toward a perception of the Nuer as a truly exotic people who live in a web of extraordinarily complex symbolic representations, an inclination that may only be augmented by Evans-Pritchard's observation that all these symbolic complexities do not faze the Nuer in the least: "Nuer pass without difficulty or hesitation from a more general and comprehensive way of conceiving of God or Spirit to a more particular and limited way of conceiving of God or Spirit and back again" (1956:52). However, Evans-Pritchard provides a key to this problem with a comment on his own fieldwork experience:

Indeed, I myself never experienced when living with the Nuer and thinking in their words and categories any difficulty commensurate with that which confronts me now when I have to translate and interpret them. I suppose I moved from representation to representation, and backwards and forwards between the general and particular, much as Nuer do and without feeling that there was any lack of co-ordination in my thoughts or that any special effort to understand was required. (1956: 106)

It would perhaps be stretching things to say that the concept *music* is like the Nuer word "*kwoth*," and yet it is unmistakably true that (1) both terms are associated with strong collective—yes, sacred— feelings, and also that (2) both terms are used, without the least uncertainty or self-consciousness, in a wide variety of senses, many of which are reciprocally contradictory. It is not only conservatory musicians but also Americans generally who move effortlessly from one to another sense or use of the word. *Nuer Religion* exemplifies the value in anthropology of focusing on variations of symbolic representation and viewing them as fundamental and essential elements of ongoing social process. One need not claim a descriptive similarity between *music* and *kwoth* in order to appropriate Evans-Pritchard's anthropological method of studying representational categories.

There appears to be no single meaning or sense of the word "music" that holds true for the numerous contexts of its use, and yet each sense of the word is characteristically used with a particularly charged intensity (as though affirming a sacred or quasisacred belief), or as an implicitly accepted *terra firma* reality. When one asks what it is that conservatory students and teachers are talking about when they refer to music, the music itself, or the actual music, one answer is that to a considerable extent they're talking about *each other*, either as individuals or as groups, formally or informally organized: they are talking about intercontextualized, configured social relationships.

When Marcus Goldmann, in coaching a young piano student, distinguished between playing the music and playing the notes, he was employing a sense of the word that is understood by everyone in the conservatory. The word *music* in such a context appears to refer to what he thought she should be feeling. That is, Goldmann's statement shows that he thought her playing was showing improper musical "feeling," even though it was clear from her comments that she herself thought that she was playing with the appropriate feeling. By the same token, when one student complained that another was "more concerned about her violin tone than about producing the music," he was using the word in nearly the same fashion, although a few sentences later when he said "to me that's what the music's indicating," the word had been recontextualized, now referring to the score, or perhaps to what he thought the score indicates.

The student who commented that orchestra players do not think of rehearsals "as being music, it's just—orchestra," gave the word a meaning on the order of something which is of value or interest, a meaning that was, of course, situated in the unpleasant social-institutional context of the tensions in the orchestra. A similar (yet not identical!) sense was given to the word by the piano student who, complaining about the dynamics surrounding the insurrection in the conservatory orchestra, remarked that the whole thing was "political," even though one couldn't prove this because, all the while, "musical" decisions were being made. This student was using the word *musical* to refer in essence to institutional or educational decisions taken to be incontestably valid and appropriate. Each of these uses of the word *music* has a referent that is unambiguously located in the social order.

As was noted earlier, more or less the same can be said of Andy Marelli's remark to his sight-singing class that "you must not think of these as music, these are drills." The word *music* in such a context refers to an idealized moral abstraction, while the context of Andy's comment consists in part of his expectations of what was to be taught and learned within the confines of that particular class; the context of the remark is, in an important sense, the conservatory's social division of educational labor. Again, much the same can be said regarding the distinction made by singers between musical matters and concerns of diction in the diction for singers class.

When Marcus Goldmann said that "music is better than the best possible performance of it," the referent of the word "music" was again an idealized abstraction, an abstraction that is closely tied to the composition. As was already noted, a composition is itself an abstraction in the sense that it exists not in any editorial version of the text, nor in any recording or any performance of it, nor in all the possible performances of it. The social burden of this sense of the word *music* is, as was also discussed earlier, clearly one that relegates the creativity of musical performance to a decidedly lower order than that of music composition.

There is another sense of the word *music* that refers to an implicitly supposed bodily substance. A conservatory violin student told me that when he auditioned for admission his teacher exclaimed to the student's mother, "My God, that boy has music!" By the same token, I remember as a child being asked "where I got my music from," and I once heard a friend complain to me that she didn't "have music." Although the anthropologist Claude Lévi-Strauss may have been indulging in rhetorical excess in referring to people who "secrete" music (Lévi-Strauss 1969: 18), such uses of the word cannot simply be dismissed out of hand as marginal, figurative, or extended senses.

Such variation suggests that the English word *music* simply does not refer to a phenomenon that exists *a priori* in the natural world. Rather, these evaluative uses serve to provide commentary on the social order. Since what music "is" is itself contingent on social situation, the inescapable conclusion is that far from being ultimately or essentially asocial in nature, music is at bottom a cultural integument of social interaction, a cultural fabric in which social process is clothed. This is not to say that music is nothing more than an elusive concept; it is, however, to say that the problematic character of the concept is a fundamental aspect of what music is. Music and "music" partake of a cultural system, a system that operates within configured social relationships.

A newspaper quotation provides an explanatory key to this problem. The passage is excerpted from a review of a concert by the famous but aging pianist Vladimir Horowitz; particular attention, of course, is called to the single appearance in this excerpt of the word *music*:

Someone remarked that Horowitz was playing like the "old Alfred Cortot." But the comparison wasn't really right. Yes, the inaccuracy and sense of physical and mental enfeeblement were the same. But when you hear those airchecks of Cortot playing Schumann and Chopin in the mid-50s, or when I recall the way I heard him play in class in 1961, there were those miraculous moments when the mists lifted, and one was suddenly in the pure presence of the music itself. With Horowitz very occasionally the mists of dubious memory and wrong notes parted, and one was in the presence of, well, Horowitz—the pianist with the unrivalled range of dynamics, from an infinite variety of pianissimo to a terrifying fortissimo that he can produce without lifting his hands higher than the Steinway colophon, the Horowitz of the peculiar musical taste, capable of fascinatingly oblique insight but seldom of direct emotional expression.[2]

Music, it seems, is something which can have a "presence." This of course raises the intriguing question of what it means to be "in the pure presence of the music," and why this is in contrast with being "in the presence of, well, Horowitz." The latter includes the "unrivalled range of dynamics" and the "fascinatingly oblique insight," but clearly neither of these is sufficient to bring the listener into the presence of "the music itself."

The allusion to the late Alfred Cortot suggests a key to one part of the problem. Among musical cognoscenti (or, at least, among an indeterminate portion of the presumed readership of this review) Cortot is remembered as a performer who in addition to having a distinctive artistic temperament manifested a scholarly concern for matters of textual interpretation.[3] In this Cortot provides a contrast with Horowitz, although the contrast should perhaps be stated in the reverse order, for Horowitz is virtually unique among still-living pianists for his willingness to add his own virtuostic embellishments to the directives in the score. The "pure presence of the music" demands a distinct quotient of circumspection from the performing artist regarding text and composer. A proper relationship of respect from the artistic performer for a revered composer is a first necessary component of "the pure presence of the music." This, of course, is dependent on the esteem in which the composer's work is held: one would never hear of "the pure presence of the music" in the case of a rendition, even by Cortot, of a technical study by Czerny.

The contrast between being in "the presence" of the music and being in "the presence" of Horowitz is related also to that between what the reviewer calls "direct emotional expression" and "peculiar musical taste." Performances by Horowitz are characterized not only by their occasional though significant deviations from the score, but also—and this more consistently—by their deviation from the normal range of variation in performance style to be found among present-day concert pianists. The "peculiar musical taste" mentioned in the review does not refer to bizarre or offbeat choices of recital repertoire (Horowitz' programs characteristically feature works by the prominent "romantic" composers—Chopin, Liszt, Schumann, and Rachmaninoff) but to style of interpretation. More than any other concert pianist living today, Horowitz' performance style diverges from that of the other leading pianists. His preeminence among pianists is certainly not a matter of unmixed praise; for many, his pianism is not simply virtuosity but also wizardry. There can be no question, moreover, that the critic contrasted being "in the presence" of Horowitz with being "in the presence" of the music in part because of the distinction of Horowitz' style from that of other established and prominent pianists. The "pure presence of the music," then, requires not only perceived indications of respect by the performer for the composer's intentions (i.e., the score), but also a perceived affinity of the performer's style with currently prevalent norms of performance. Such can be taken as a second criterion for being in the "pure presence of the music." In spite of the tremendous importance musicians place on artistic individualism, artistic individuality can be perceived as excessive. Horowitz' unique style runs for him the risk of being considered idiosyncratic or, as in the opinion of the present critic, "peculiar."

Of course, not everyone agrees with Horowitz' detractors, a fact which brings a third variable into the social configuration requisite of "the pure presence of the music." The matter of whether or not the performer has manifested an adequate respect for the composer and is sufficiently in keeping with pervading norms of performance is inevitably and necessarily interpreted by a listener, a critic, a commentator—and of course commentators are in fact no less likely than pianists to be idiosyncratic or to have "peculiar taste." While I do not accept the idea that there is no accounting for taste, there can be no denying the fact that taste is variable, and what for one critic seems to be the "pure presence of the music" might seem quite different—pure schmaltz, perhaps, or pedantic nonsense—to someone else. Whatever the critic was referring to, however, with his expression "the pure presence of the music itself," its reality is constituted in relationships among a configuration of persons embodying particular roles—that is, among composers, performers, and listener-critics. Thus a third criterion of arriving at a "pure presence of the music" is a shared understanding of interpretive style between the performer and the critic.

# The Role Set and the Art World

The preceding analysis of the "presence of the music" is inspired in part by an analytical model presented in Wyatt MacGaffey's comparative study of African religious systems (1980). In this article MacGaffey makes the point that "the principle of comparative work, that only sets of elements can be compared and not elements in isolation, has long been accepted in kinship studies" (1980: 304), and he goes on to argue that such a principle should be equally applicable to the study of religion since, as he noted, "it is futile to reify an abstraction we call religion and then ask what its relations are to other abstractions we call government or economy" (1980: 322).

The observation that provides the basis for MacGaffey's discussion is that although both the Azande and the BaKongo of Africa are presented in the anthropological literature as having, or believing in, witchcraft, the fact is that Zande "witches" are utterly dissimilar from BaKongo "witches." It is the English word "witchcraft" that constitutes the primary element the two phenomena have in common (1980: 301–305). MacGaffey contends that what is or is not called "witchcraft" in anthropology is less important than the means by which such spiritual beings are believed to operate and be controlled. MacGaffey notes that African belief systems characteristically include particular configurations of supernatural beings, and that the powers of supernatural beings are characteristically understood as complemented and contrasted, or constrained and controlled, by those of other beings within this supernatural configuration. As such, MacGaffey points out, these configurations take on characteristics of a mode of production. MacGaffey applied the phrase "role sets" to these modes of spiritual production.

It would be both impossible and unwise to superimpose MacGaffey's analysis, whole cloth, onto an analysis of music. MacGaffey's analysis dealt with sets of religious beings, mine with configurations of actual persons. Moreover, the notion of role risks bringing with it a confusing collection of theoretical anachronisms regarding the nature of social structure.[4] Nevertheless, MacGaffey's insight is unquestionably appropriate to the present discussion, and his notion of role set lends itself to the problem of conceiving a configuration, an organization, of the multiplicity of contexts in which music is made—a metacontext.

The notions of *role* and *role set* focus analytical attention on the musicians and the social configurations involved in music making, rather than rely on received conceptions of music or musical structure.

Musical activity is both organized and evaluated with respect to relatively well understood role expectations, for example that of the performer's respect for the composer requisite of the "pure presence of the music" discussed earlier. An evaluation of music is almost always an evaluation of social action or a comment on social ranking. A statement that a student did not play with the proper "feeling" is ultimately a sincerity judgment; a statement that a teacher's comments are "destructive" comments on the teacher's presumed values and social sensitivity; saying that the composer of the piece in question was a "genius" comments on social ranking. Here again one sees directly the validity of Leach's formulation regarding the identification of ethics and esthetics. Notions of role, however implicit and context-specific, can be inferred as being pertinent to nearly all musical evaluations in a conservatory.

What is called classical music is by and large produced in a role set, or social configuration, consisting of composer, performer, and audience; teacher and pupil; and also music critic, musicologist, and music theorist. Of course, the division of musical labor is in fact considerably more complex than this; my "performers" category glosses over important distinctions between soloists and accompanists, conductors and orchestra members, prima donnas and chorus members. Even more important, music is hardly produced in a "set" environment; it is, rather, produced in an evolving social configuration. However, even as outlined in this foreshortened form, there are specific and collectively understood values and behavioral expectations that pertain to this configuration of generalized roles.

As the previous chapter showed, there is an intensely sacralized distance between the performer and the audience at a recital or concert of classical music. The ritual silence of the audience at such events is in effect the honoring of a taboo against talking, singing, dancing, and eating or drinking. Lest this be taken as unduly trivial, however, it should be pointed out that just such activities, singing, dancing, eating, and drinking, are completely acceptable, and sometimes almost obligatory, as accompaniment to music in other contexts. The taboo in classical music against such behavior is, of course, a function of the fact that a recital is a ritual in which individual performers can manifest themselves as specially, perhaps uniquely, gifted interpreters of musical texts; in such contexts, talking, dancing, or eating would of course constitute an utterly unacceptable distraction. The role-specific nature of this ritual silence can be seen in the fact that the taboo on speaking is not applied to particular persons, but rather to any person attending the performance as—that is to say, in the role of—audience member.

Someone who insisted upon talking audibly during a recital performance of a Mozart sonata would be violating the normative behavior of the audience-member role just as a man who squandered his daughter's weekly allowance on gambling would be violating normative behavior of the father role. It should be remembered that in several of the recitals I attended, the soloist's family made up a sizeable percentage of what was a very small audience; the taboo against speaking was in effect against parents and strangers alike. Of course, the taboo against talking pertains also to the performer, a fact that puts the classical music recitalist in sharp contrast with the jazz or folk musician who characteristically generates a considerable amount of "patter" in the performance context, talking, sometimes at some length, about the songs, their social context, his or her own personal reason for singing the song, and the like.

It should not be glossed over that in the context of classical music the activity of contemplative listening is given a very special significance. Many colleges and universities—even those that do not offer courses in the composing or performing of music—offer what are in fact courses on listening under the title "music appreciation." Aaron Copland's *What to Listen for in Music* is something of a bible in this area, and there are several texts (e.g., Kerman 1980, Nadeau and Tesson 1981), whose titles are one-word directives: *Listen*.

In addition to the separation between performer and listener, there is a similarly sacralized distance between the roles of performer and composer. It is here that we encounter the criterion of respect from the performer for the composer, mentioned previously in connection with the Horowitz review and the "pure presence of the music." Typically—and in at least one sense of the word, ideally—composers are dead, and a score is treated, as a matter of reverence and respect, somewhat as one treats a will. Even in the case of a living composer, the score is a script whose directives are not, ideally, to be violated. Accordingly, improvising is viewed as disrespectful and is forbidden. Indeed, if you improvise, then you're not "really" playing Beethoven, or doing what the music says to do. Improvising while playing Beethoven, like talking in the audience, would clearly be a violation of a well-defined musical role. Both in spite and because of the strong ritual frame of formal recitals, within this idiom real musical "creativity" is perceived as emanating solely from the composer role. One occasionally hears in the conservatory the use of the word *re-creative* to characterize the art of musical performance. Significantly, the notion of "genius" is used almost solely with reference to the composer role.

In other musical contexts such is not the case at all. For example, the separation between the roles of composer and performer is much less prominent in jazz, and in much of what is considered "blues," the role of composer is virtually nonexistent (see Keil 1966 for a valuable discussion of the interplay of the roles of blues singer and preacher in urban Afro-American culture). In neither of these idioms is there a stricture against improvisation. Indeed, for many people, if you *don't* improvise, it's not really jazz.

As was discussed in Chapter Two, pedagogical lineages are important elements in the social organization of the conservatory, and the formal teacher-student pairing must be considered as a fundamental element in the production of Western art music. One simply cannot, does not, and will not become a "classical" musician through only informal learning. The expectations of formal training, of course, distinguish this musical idiom from other idioms in which there is no formal teaching, and in which musicians may never learn to read musical notation. In such musical idioms, performers may be less likely to be identified with their past or present musical mentors—conservatory teachers, it will be recalled, were identified as students of Schnabel or Piatigorsky—than with prominent performers they have played with. Jazz players are characteristically billed as having performed with, say, Sonny Rollins or Dizzy Gillespie.

Of course, a jazz musician billed as having played with a Sonny Rollins is in all probability one who effectively became a student or an apprentice of the jazz master. The significant difference here lies in the fact that in an unwritten idiom such as jazz, the method of musical pedagogy can hardly be formalized lessons in which master instructs pupil, but rather sessions in which learner and teacher play together. Thus the cultural authority of the printed text/score in classical music is intertwined with the institution of formalized teacher-pupil dyads. Here again we see the significance of the multiplicity of contexts that are at issue in musical production.

Music critics, musicologists, and music theorists all play important though varied roles in this musical idiom, roles that, once again, characterize the present role set and contrast it with that of other musical idioms. Music critics, for example, generally write for daily newspapers and periodicals, producing written evaluations of musical performers and performances. From such a vantage point they hold some power over the fortunes of performers, and there is an undeniable tension between the performer and critic roles. From performing musicians one occasionally hears complaints to the effect that "music critics are usually not trained musicians, but are only gross amateurs or nonmusicians entirely." Whether or not one thinks that bad critics are more harmful to musical standards than bad performers, there can be no doubting the fact that critics and performers draw on different sources of authentication. It is also important to remember that only in recent years[5] have the music pages of major newspapers included reviews of public performances of various kinds of "popular" music.

By contrast with critics, music theorists characteristically teach in colleges and universities and write for formal academic publications; they produce analytic models that are characteristically based on studies of compositions—texts—to the exclusion of performance. The distinction between "music" and "performance" can be linked to the distinction between the theorist and the critic: the roles involved in the musical production are differentially associated with the various concepts that are at issue in classical music.

It seems to me that the role set notion could provide a framework for comparisons of various musical idioms as well as for looking at the ways in which communicative resources and social values are distributed and redistributed. For example, the proximity that has in the twentieth century been manifested between the role of composer and that of music theorist (as in the cases, for example, of Schoenberg, Hindemith, and Babbitt, all of whom achieved prominence both as composers and theorists, but not as performers) constitutes a significant shift from the earlier proximity between the roles of composer and performer (as with Mozart, Beethoven, and Liszt, all of whom were great performers and composers but not theorists). Similarly, the effective prohibition of improvisation in present-day performances of Mozart contrasts with the apparently widespread practise of improvisatory embellishments in performances of Mozart's compositions during the composer's lifetime.

Moreover, in an age of electronic communication it is perhaps inevitable that the social authority that can be encapsulated in the printed score would be threatened. In this connection, some of the innovation by present-day composers of "new music" lies apparently in its reorganization of the division of musical labor, its changing of the role set by supplementing or replacing the score and the interpreter/performer with, for example, an electronic synthesizer and prerecorded tape. Other "new" compositions, by contrast, might be viewed as culturally retrospective, to the extent that they draw on the authority of the written score and thus retain an orientation toward the composer-performer schism of the preceding role set.

The Eastern Metropolitan Conservatory also exemplifies an important portion of what sociologist Howard Becker would call the "art world" of Western art music (Becker 1982). Becker defines an *art world* as "the network of people whose cooperative activity, organized via their joint knowledge of conventional means of doing things, produces the kind of art works that art world is noted for" (Becker 1982: x). The major thrust of Becker's study is to call attention to the active and productive nature of the numerous people who make up an art world network. Nevertheless, Becker frames his analysis with a significant qualification, one that postulates an analytical schism between two senses of the word *work*:

> The dominant position [of the sociology of art] takes the artist and art work, rather than the network of cooperation, as central to the analysis of art as a social phenomenon. In light of this difference, it might be reasonable to say that what I have done here is not the sociology of art at all, but rather the sociology of occupations applied to artistic work. I would not quarrel with that way of putting it. (Becker 1982: xi)

Becker's confession posits a distinction between "the art work" (*qua* product) and "artistic work" (*qua* productivity). However since, as was already noted, a work of music (such as a Beethovan quartet) cannot be equated with its score, or with a performance of it, or with the skills requisite to playing it, this work exists only in the abstract, and its production cannot be simply extricated from the production of the evaluative concepts with which it is received. What is and is not the actual music, the actual piece, the actual composition, is a matter of social negotiation—occasionally easy consensus, but frequently contentious negotiation. Again, a musical work of art is not an objectively found datum available for formal study in some socially neutral fashion.

Perhaps significantly, such is not the case with some of the other art media: there is an actual *Mona Lisa*, and a very real Brooklyn

Bridge, each of which is utterly singular, with a concrete reality that cannot be compromised, for example, by the proliferation of photographic reproductions of them (although their social and esthetic meanings, of course, are very much compromised in this fashion). Such is simply not the case with the *Eroica* symphony or the *Well-Tempered Clavier*. A given performance or published edition of the score may well be taken as "being" the *Eroica*, but nobody thinks that the *Eroica is* that performance or edition. However real it is, the *Eroica* symphony is an abstraction. The Brooklyn Bridge, however, is the Brooklyn Bridge.

That said, I hasten to add that the points of analytical difference between the *Eroica* symphony and the Brooklyn Bridge are in this context less crucial than their similarities, for my basic emendation to Becker's presentation would be to insist that cultural abstractions (the *Eroica* symphony) are, no less than material constructions (the Brooklyn Bridge), themselves products, produced by a network of social actors. While I take it as self-evident that nobody would deny that the *Eroica* symphony is a "work" that was and is produced through individual and collective activity (just as was the Brooklyn Bridge), calling attention to the ultimately abstract nature of the *Eroica* should facilitate an understanding of the socially produced character of other cultural abstractions—including also concepts such as music, art, and various other terms of esthetic evaluation.

# Figurative Diction in Theoretical Accounts

The socially produced nature of cultural abstractions can be seen also in the concepts that are at issue in the writings of music theorists, perhaps particularly in these theorists' conceptions of music. In this, an element of historical perspective will be of help, since what we today call classical music is generally characterized as something with a very long historical tradition. Music history is one of the predominant perspectives on Western art music, and students study this music as something handed down, not only from the times of Beethoven and Bach, but before that from Palestrina, Josquin, Machaut, Pope Gregory I, and classical antiquity.

Two points are worth mention here. First, the idea that music is something that has been "handed down" has not always been held, even within this very history of music (Allen 1962: 3–28). Second, conceptions of music dating from earlier historical eras, though now presented as part of the heritage of Western musical culture, are arguably as different from contemporary Western musical conceptions as these are from some of the non-Western "other" cultures that are often made the topic of anthropological or ethnomusicological study. For example, the idea of music based in the harmonic workings of the cosmos, the "music of the spheres," an idea that was the starting point of music theory in medieval Europe, seems no less strange than the idea that music originated with a god named Efile Mukulu, and was transmitted through a culture hero named Mulopwe, which according to Merriam (1964: 74) is the belief of the Basongye of Zaire.[6]

It may not be an altogether fruitless fantasy to ask how present-day conceptions of music might have appeared to people of earlier times. An insightful comment in this regard comes from Jean-Jacques Nattiez, who, in discussing the total avoidance of verbal meaning that characterizes twentieth-century theories of music, notes that

> This has not always been the case in music's history. When Fontenelle apostrophizes: *"sonate, que me veux-tu?"* [sonata, what do you want from me?] his question is symptomatic of the disarray in which the theorists of the classical period were thrown when they found themselves confronted with the dilemma of pure instrumental music. (Nattiez 1977: 126)

It is perhaps only a truism that cultural change is a form of cultural diversity. However, the use of figurative language in interpreting problematic cultural forms has, it seems to me, a significance even beyond that suggested by Nattiez. For while Nattiez noted the device of apostrophe specifically in connection with an important cultural innovation (purely instrumental music: sonatas), contemporary music theory is rather generally characterized by systematic use of figurative language.

Of course, purely instrumental music is obviously no longer a source of "disarray" for music theorists. On the contrary, for many theorists, instrumental music exemplifies the essence of what music is. The nineteenth-century critic Eduard Hanslick, for example, equated instrumental music with music itself: "only what is true of [instrumental music] is true of music as such . . . [instrumental music] alone is true and self-subsistent music" (Hanslick 1957 [1891]: 29–30). In this Hanslick was only articulating the postulate that has informed music theory for over a century. What may be less obvious, however, is the extent to which modern music theory employs figurative language in operationalizing the concept of "music."

For example, Heinrich Schenker, one of the most influential music theorists of this century, was adamant regarding the importance of anthropomorphic thinking in music theory: "we should get accustomed to seeing tones as creatures. We should learn to assume in them biological urges as they characterize living beings" (Schenker 1954 [1906]: 6). Schenker repeatedly referred to the "egotism" of musical tones, and argued, for example, that "the motif lives through its fate, like a personage in a drama" (1954: 13).

A different but no less anthropomorphic style of presentation can be seen in Leonard B. Meyer's well-known analysis of musical meaning (1956). Meyer states, for example, that "in following and responding to the sound gestures made by the composer, the listener may become oblivious of his own ego, which has literally become one with that of the music" (1956: 41). In this formulation Meyer has produced a powerfully configured conception of what "music" is, an anthropomorphic conception in which "music" has an ego, one with which the listener's ego can "become one." The fact that it is the performer and not the composer who makes the actual sounds might in some contexts seem obvious if not banal, but in this case it is of considerable import, since the listener's ego is said to become one with that of a music conceived as composer's design plus performers' sounds, these already "one" with each other.

Meyer says that this is to be taken "literally," and it might seem that in unpacking his formulation in the preceding fashion I have declined to do so. On the other hand, there is a very significant question of just what it would mean to interpret such a statement literally. I for one take it to be the case that there is a ("literal") sense in which a person has an ego but music does not, and that only in a figurative sense could music be said to have an ego. Nevertheless, there is more than a little understanding to be gained from taking Meyer at his word and at least acquiescing to the idea that music really does have an ego. The understanding to be gained is precisely this: in the bulk of contemporary theoretical texts, music is not so much an entity occasionally described with anthropomorphic terms as it is itself an anthropomorphic, figurative representation.

Since one of the points I am trying to make is that the word *music* is an essential part but not the entirety of what music is, it should perhaps be emphasized that the absence of quotation marks around the word "music" in the previous sentence is neither accidental nor insignificant. It is not the word, but rather that which music is taken to be, that is characteristically anthropomorphized in the discourse of music theory. Consider, for example, a clause such as "the instrumental line persists with single-mindedness on its sequential way" (Meyer 1956: 98), an anthropomorphic statement that unambiguously refers to music without using the word, "music." In this instance it might seem that it is the phrase "with single-mindedness" that provides the element of anthropomorphism in this expression, in that one might think of persons but not instrumental lines as potentially "single-minded."

Remove it, however, and we are left with "the instrumental line persists on its sequential way," a statement hardly less anthropomorphic, although now seemingly because of the verb "persists." Changing the verb, for example, to "goes" only calls attention to the anthropomorphic element in "on its sequential way." Thus it is not only particular words and phrases that are anthropomorphic, but the whole manner of conceiving the subject matter.

For a different kind of example, consider Meyer's comment that in the second movement of the "Eroica" symphony "the B-flat in measure twenty disturbs the established sequence by entering one beat earlier than expected" (1956: 125). This statement not only lacks the word "music," but also lacks a personality-characterizing modifier such as the "single-mindedly" in the previous example. However, it is no less anthropomorphic in nature. One would alter the particulars but not the tone of this statement by inserting an anthropomorphized adverb such as "rudely" or "courageously" before the word "disturbs." The anthropomorphic sense of the expression is manifested independently of such words.

Nor are Meyer and Schenker exceptional in their use of anthropomorphic language in presenting musical analyses. Arnold Schoenberg, another major theorist of the present century, classified certain kinds of harmonies as "vagrant" and others as "roving." Even Hanslick, whose place in music history was secured largely in connection with his insistence that concrete human emotions cannot be attributed to music, made a point of allowing that music can be characterized as "graceful, gentle, violent, vigorous, elegant, [and] fresh" (Hanslick 1957: 23).

In many texts written by music theorists, then, music is a fiction—not in the sense of being a falsehood, a deception, or even other than real, but rather in the sense that what music is is at least partially created in and by the texts that analyze it. The figurative language with which music theorists represent the abstraction called "music" is of fundamental importance in understanding what this abstraction is.

Of course, anthropomorphism is hardly the only type of figurative language employed in theoretical narratives. Schoenberg, for example, makes liberal use of spatial images such as harmonic "regions," "centrifugal" and "centripetal" harmonic tendencies, and "gliding" chords. In a similar vein, classes in musical analysis almost everywhere contend with problems of "form": sonata "form," rondo "form," and binary "form" (the figurative character of the word *form* was noted satirically by the French composer Erik Satie when he composed "Three Pieces in the Form of a Pear"). Any number of similar examples could readily be found. However, surely the most important kind of figurative language in music theory—one might be tempted to say "apart from anthropomorphism" except for the fact that it works in tandem with anthropomorphic language—is synecdoche, the presenting of part as though the whole.

One sense in which music theory can be said to be synecdochical is in its associating instrumental music with music itself, or music *per se*. The more important and pervading synecdoche, however, is in the avoidance by music theorists of issues of musical performance, and studying as "music" only those issues that pertain to the structure or organization of compositions. In this once again, Hanslick provided the model: "from a philosophical point of view, a composition is the finished work of art, irrespective of its performance" (Hanslick 1957: 75). A fundamental opposition between music and performance has been, at least since Hanslick's time, nothing less than a first principle in the theoretical study of music.

To be sure, compositions surely provide both an appropriate unit of analysis and a valid object of inquiry. On the other hand, it is one thing to generate a theoretical approach to the study of compositions, and quite another to construe this as a theory of "music." Something very much like this is the case with modern music theory. The nature of the problem is illustrated by noting that the same Hanslick who said that the composition is the complete work of musical art also said that "the essence of music is sound and motion" (1957: 48). The significance of this lies in the fact that both musical sound and musical motion are manifested specifically in performance: when isolated from performance, the characteristics of a musical composition are not sound and motion but silence and stillness on the printed pages of the score.

The analytical import of synecdoche in music theory texts, then, is precisely this: music theoretical accounts typically presume various effects that are specific to performance (e.g., sound and motion) without contending with its contingent circumstances (the social frame of performance or variations of performing style and skill). Viewed in the context of the polymorphic nature of music and the social production of cultural abstractions, what is of significance is not so much the internally contradictory nature of music theoretical formulations as the fact that such formulations have been produced in connection with a figurative way of representing "music" itself.

If Hanslick had argued, for example, that the printed pages of a musical score are incapable of producing concrete human feeling, it seems more than likely that nobody would have paid much attention; such would surely have been granted as self-evident. Hanslick, however, argued that it was *music* that is incapable of expressing human feeling. Here logic goes in contrary directions: to the extent that "music" is logically coterminous with the composer's silent text ("a composition is the finished work of art"), it is a banality to say that music (*qua* texts) cannot express human feelings. However, if "music" is "sound and motion," then saying that music is incapable of expressing human feelings, as Hanslick did, can be a very unsettling proposition.[7] It was, of course, taken as such. It seems at least arguable that the intense controversy that greeted Hanslick's formulations was at bottom a social adjustment to a powerful cultural innovation, namely the figurative, anthropomorphic-synecdochical representation of what music is. That such a figural representation has been accepted by contemporary music theorists seems attested, for example, by the unassuming confidence with which Meyer could refer to "the sound gestures of the composer" and the "ego" of the music.

# Production and Experience

The point of this discussion of synecdoche, anthropomorphism, and the other figurative devices that manifest themselves in the texts of music theory—as well as the categorization of music theory as in large part a "fiction"—is intended less to show music theory as simply a type of literature than to characterize it as a type of symbolic action. Figurative writing is by no means the exclusive province of novelists and poets, and procedures adapted from literary analysis are not limited in their validity to the study of the *belles letters*.[8]

Traditional musicological wisdom would have it that sociological issues must inevitably remain at the periphery of analyses of music itself. Such a view, however, ideologically overlooks the fundamental musical importance of performers and teachers of music. I have called this view into question by focusing attention on the activities of performers and teachers of music, as well as on the concept of "music itself." The role set, or art world, or mode of musical production that has been schematized here is not simply a social context within which an acoustical phenomenon called "music" is made. A musical role set or art world is not only a mode of musical production; it is at the same time a mode of musical experience. The concepts and values engendered in the present role set include a contextually shifting sense of what "music" is. As was discussed in Chapter Five, just as the sacred entails the secular, music entails nonmusic. What is music in one context is inevitably nonmusic in another; what is music for one person is inevitably nonmusic for someone else; and what is music in one sense of the term is systematically construed as nonmusic in other senses of the word.

Music is not an *a priori* phenomenon of the natural world. Neither is it a unitary entity, nor a single bounded domain. Music— "music"—is a cultural system, an intercontextualized weave of conceptual representations, actions and reactions, ideas and feelings, sounds and meanings, values and structures. None of these elements can alone be taken as constituting the core or the essence of music, for the simple reason that in the ongoing flow of day to day life, whether inside or outside the conservatory, any of these aspects of music is available on an instant's notice to be invoked, presented, or experienced as the essence of music, the "actual" music, the music "itself."

A historical musicologist or a music theorist might reply to all of this that I have been indulging in a game of words, seizing and expanding upon marginal uses of the term. Such a comment would not be without validity. In the present study I have been producing my own anthropological and somewhat semiotic conception of music, basing this conception on both my observations of conservatory life and my reading of musicological literature. My conception of music is indeed a product of both my personal experience and my research. This fact, however, is only a particular instance of the more general point, namely that conceptions of music are by nature products of social actors in social situations. Music theorists produce and reproduce anthropomorphic and synecdochical conceptions of music in the context of structural studies of compositions, and the students and teachers at EMCM continually produce and reproduce musical conceptions in contexts where the notion is highly evaluative and negotiable. Music does indeed have formal rules; however, these rules are not applied formally. Rather, they are negotiated, invoked, and appealed to in various social contexts. Musical forms are continually transmuted by social forms.

My argument regarding the cultural production of musical experience is consonant with a discussion of "production forces" made by Raymond Williams. Although the context of Williams' discussion is a study of literature, one comment on musical productivity is particularly germane to my present argument. Williams quite rightly criticizes a statement of Karl Marx that although a piano maker engages in productive work, a pianist does not (Williams 1977: 93). As Williams notes, the fact that some pianists do in fact produce directly for the market (i.e., commercial recordings and concerts) is only part of the difficulty: "if 'production', in capitalist society, is the production of commodities for a market, then different but misleading terms are found for every other kind of production and productive force" (1977: 92–93).

Williams' point (or at least, the part of his point that I want to appropriate) is that a product is truly a cultural product not because it is marketable but because it is meaningful. A piano is a marketable product, but only because people know what a piano is and is for, and because someone may, in this knowledge, want to buy one. Cultural meaning is a necessary element in any marketable product. Even though not all cultural meaning is marketable, this is inadequate as a basis for claiming that only that which is marketable (a piano, for example, perhaps with attention to the difference between a Steinway and a Yamaha) deserves to be considered as a product. John Doe's piano playing is a cultural product, even though he may not, like Horowitz, "produce" his pianism for the marketplace. Jane Doe's musical feelings and opinions are similarly a cultural product, even if she does not "produce" them, say, for the music page of a newspaper.

In all of this I should stress that I am not attempting to say that music does not really exist, or to reduce music to social interaction. Music is real—I experience it as real, and I know nobody who does not experience it as real. My argument is that the essence of music is not in its structure, not in its sounds, nor its meaning or the feelings it arouses, although all of these are both real and important. Music cannot be reduced, for example, to "humanly organized sound" (Blacking 1973: 3), however appealing the phrase. The financier-composer Charles Ives was not just being mystical in his warnings against paying too much attention to the sound lest we miss out on the music (e.g., Ives 1962: 168). The fact that "organized sound" can be a rather fractious, troublesome element of music is also suggested by books about music with titles such as *Silence* (Cage 1971) and *Noise* (Attali 1985).

My argument, rather, is that music entails a cultural system, a system of various and yet interdependent representations. A cultural system, moreover, is produced and reproduced, interpreted and reinterpreted, both continually and intermittently, in social configurations, whether they be called webs of meaning, contexts, role sets, or art worlds. The essence of music as a cultural system is both that it is *not* an *a priori* phenomenon of the natural world and also that *it is experienced as though it were*, as though nothing could be more concrete, natural, or phenomenal.[9] The essence of music as a cultural system lies in the fact that music is a cultural integument of social activity.

The Western cultural experience is that music is a perceptible reality: anybody knows that we can hear music, and that when we hear it, it can have a strong impact on us—we feel it. Nevertheless, it is not trivial to point out that what one hears is not music but sounds. The perception of music is an interpretive response to—one could equally say, a responsive interpretation of—the hearing of particular tones and other sounds. The perception of music is a fundamentally cultural activity, and never simply a physiological or neurophysiological processing of accoustical events.

# Postscript

When I began my studies of anthropology, my goal was to investigate the extent to which Western art music could be said to be a metaphoric representation of the social processes in which it takes place. My research, however, has not convinced me that music either is or is not a metaphoric representation of society so much as it has forced upon me an awareness of the persistently figurative nature of language, and of symbolic action generally. For example, if one takes the essence of metaphor to be the contrast between literal and figurative diction, then a sentence such as "her cheek was a red rose" is metaphoric precisely because cheeks and roses belong to distinct and separate domains. However, the problem of the simultaneously literal and metaphoric nature of the "ego" of the music reveals the limitations of such a conception of metaphor. My present discomfort with the notion of music as a metaphoric representation of social process is tied to my conclusion that neither music nor social process is a concrete, closed, or bounded system: on the contrary, each is informed by the other, and the process through which this takes place is itself heavily informed with metaphor (Lakoff and Johnson 1980, de Man 1978).

Problems of cultural analysis have also frequently been discussed in terms of "reflection," that is, the idea that one cultural domain (music or language) can be seen to "reflect" characteristics of another domain (social structure or thought processes). Still other approaches have been based on the idea that one domain constitutes the "codification" of a second domain. To my way of thinking, such formulations entail domains that tend to be clearly distinguishable only in the abstraction of analysis (that is, they are at least in part created—constituted—in these analytical texts), and part of the problem is the related fact that grounding analysis on such abstract domains forecloses on the possibility of basing analysis on the ongoing flux of social practise. As Williams notes, the concept of " 'code' has a further irony, in that it implies, somewhere, the existence of the same message 'in clear'" (Williams 1977: 169; on the other hand, for a formidable musical analysis in terms of the "coding of ideologies," see Shepherd et al. 1977: 69–124).

Characterizing music in terms of a cultural system provides a corrective for the idea that music is an objective and phenomenal reality of the natural world. Such a characterization focuses on the fact that the nature of a musical system is neither closed nor formal, nor governed solely by its own internal laws or rules, but rather is modified, maintained, and reproduced in the varied contexts of an ongoing flow of symbolic action.

# NOTES

## CHAPTER ONE

1. Throughout this book I have given pseudonyms to all persons and institutions with whom I have been personally associated.

2. In a paper presented at the 1984 meeting of the Society for Ethnomusicology, Stephen Blum (1984) gave an instructive discussion of the uses and implications of this concept. Significantly, many of Blum's references are to German scholars, notably Dalhaus' *Die Idee der absoluten Music* (1978). However, the widespread currency of the term is indicated by its appearance in theoretical texts such as Cone's *Musical Form and Musical Performance* (1967: 21), as well as more "popular" texts such as Spaeth's *The Art of Enjoying Music* (1949: 179–180) and Machlis' *The Enjoyment of Music* (1963: 137–169).

3. Cf. Chapter Six, note number 5.

4. This is not to imply, of course, that the configuration is confined to these six elements. For example, the roles of recording companies, radio, television, video, government, and philanthropic foundations are hardly unimportant, and much work needs to be done if we are to understand the interplay between economic competition and philanthropic benefaction in musical culture. That, however, must be another study.

5. For a more extensive discussion of the role of administrative assistants in an arts school, see Adler (1979).

6. Bourdieu is quite explicit regarding the risks entailed in claiming to make explicit the practical (i.e., inexplicit) aspects of social action. He suggests an "everything happens as if" qualifier to analytic descriptions as a reminder of "the epistemological status of the constructed concepts of objective science," and as precaution against "the reifying of concepts and of theoretical constructs" (Bourdieu 1977: 203). Similar warnings regarding "God's truth" claims in anthropology can be inferred from Geertz's remark that anthropological analysis is a fiction (1973: 15f.), or from Wagner's (1981) position that the anthropologists' "culture" is an "intervention."

7. This discussion draws extensively on Giddens (1976).

## CHAPTER TWO

1. The reason for this should not be laid purely to a supposed indifference to students, but rather to a conservatory-wide idea that teachers are not only artistic individuals but also individualistic artists.

2. The fact that the analysis in anthropology of systems of political patronage has centered on systems characterized by violence and corruption (cf. Campbell 1964, Boissevain 1966, Blok 1974) should not make such a suggestion appear incongruous. The point is to suggest a structural similarity between systems based on the linking of esteem and authority.

3. Of course, the stigma attached to the word "clique" may make any such characterization seem incongruous. My point is that a single type of social grouping is interpreted in conflicting ways. To clarify this point, it might help to say that in conservatory parlance, a group that might be referred to as "their clique" by an outsider might more likely be referred to as "our studio" by an insider.

4. Readers who have seen the movie "The Competition" may remember the enumeration of this very lineage by one of the characters in that film. I can only assert that my own anecdote was not borrowed from the film, and that the incident in the film speaks to the general significance of not only that particular pedagogical line, but also of such lineages in general.

5. Perhaps the most prominent work on the nature of aural tradition is Albert Lord's *The Singer of Tales* (1960), in which performance context is shown to replace narrative text as the determining agency in the organization of oral poetry. Ethnomusicologists focusing on the central importance of aural tradition are simply too numerous to mention, but I should perhaps point out that Ben Sidran's *Black Talk* (1971), which made such an impression on me when I first read it, was based to a great extent on the theories of nonliterate culture of Marshall McLuhan.

6. This is an examination administered shortly before required degree recitals.

7. Seating in the orchestra is not only a matter of prestige but also in many cases a matter of the difference between playing or staying silent in certain solo passages.

8. The number of woodwind, brass, and percussion players in the orchestra varies greatly from piece to piece, so that setting up the orchestra requires knowledge of the repertoire scheduled for rehearsal.

9. Also significant in this connection is the fact that wind players in the orchestra generally play one to a part, while each string player is but one of a large section.

## CHAPTER THREE

1. The parallel with the literary notion of "intertextuality" is intentional.

2. There is, of course, a substantial body of literature dealing with the psychology of musical ability and music aptitude testing. Bridges (1965) concludes her survey of such studies with a remark that seems to invite analyses such as my own: "when somebody finds the answer to that enigmatical question 'what is musicality?' perhaps the problem will be at least half-solved" (1965: 59). For a somewhat more recent compendium, see Critchley and Henson (1977). This is a reader that deals with numerous neurological matters, but again, few of the findings are dramatic. R. T. C. Pratt's observation on inheritance is representative: "the scientific study of the inheritance of musicality offers particular difficulties, and no firm conclusions can be reached at the present time" (1977: 22). In a somewhat contrasting vein, neurologist Frank R. Wilson has recently argued that "all of us have a biologic guarantee of musicianship. . . . We all have music inside us, and can learn to get it out, one way or another. We are natural musicians because of the special nature of the human brain and the phenomenal muscular system to which it is attached" (Wilson 1986: 2).

3. The anthropological term for this is *segmentation*, a concept that has historically been associated with lineage and kinship systems of social and political organization (Evans-Pritchard 1940, Fortes 1945, 1949, Smith 1956). The point of interest in the present analysis of "talent" is that the unit of segmentation here extends to inner traits of particular persons (cf. also Herzfeld 1984; I am indebted to Michael Herzfeld for numerous valuable discussions on, among other things, the topic of segmentation).

4. This point draws on R. D. Laing's discussion (1961: 151–173) of attributions and injunctions.

5. The phrase "tin ear" is of course metaphorical, except perhaps when used in reference to a certain woodman from the land of Oz. Perhaps less obvious, however, is the metaphoric nature of the phrase "tone-deaf." It deserves to be said out loud that "tone deafness" is not a particular kind of deafness, nor a physiological defect in a person's auditory system. Nobody can be considered physiologically "tone-deaf," for example, if they can both perceive and produce the subtleties of vocal tone through which so much is conveyed in speech. Nevertheless, "tone deafness" is treated as though an objective phenomenon in a great deal of everyday talk about music, and the proximate notion of "tune-deaf" has been given a certain degree of serious attention in scholarly literature, sometimes under its own Latin taxonomic name, *dismelodia* (Kalmus and Fry 1980: 369). Zuckerkandl, for example, holds that

when a tune-deaf person listens to a melody, he hears tones succeeding one another; he does not hear melody. He hears music as we hear a lecture in a language we do not understand. The tones themselves, the sound, he perceives exactly as the normal person does; he lacks the organ [sic] for the *meaning* in the tones. (1956: 16, emphasis original)

6. The quotation is from the *Standard Revised Version*. The conclusion of the parable is provocatively explicit: to the servant who refused to invest the talent given him, the master replies,

You wicked and slothful servant! You knew that I reap where I have not sowed, and gather where I have not winnowed? Then you ought to have invested my money with the bankers, and at my coming I would have received what was my own with interest. So take the talent from him, and give it to him who has the ten talents. For to every one who has will more be given, and he will have abundance; but from him who has not, even what he has will be taken away.

It may not be superfluous to add that the more recent New English Bible, while dropping the word *talent*, has replaced the word *property* with *capital*.

7. Of course, the biblical parable also points up the metaphoric character of the word *talent* as characterization of special abilities, such as in music. The metaphoric basis of musical talk and writing will be discussed again in the concluding chapter.

8. This point is essentially the same as the analyses of the political and emotional factors involved in bowling performance by Whyte (1955: 19–23) and in verbal performance by Labov (1972: 331).

9. It is at least possible that linguistic competence also is contingent upon factors of emotionally supportive social environment. Such an hypothesis is implied in anthropologist Jean Briggs's account of her fieldwork in an Eskimo family. Briggs recounts that she had lived among the Eskimos for a full year when she was subtly but effectively ostracized for a period of three months. During this interval she experienced a severe and fatiguing depression; she was both confused and distressed. "Moreover," she points out, "my intense resentment at the unpleasant situation resulted in a spectacular decline in my own linguistic prowess. I could not remember even the simplest words, which had become second nature to me" (Briggs 1970: 3; see also 274–307). When finally there was a reconciliation, Briggs began to regain her speaking competence: "my vocabulary unfroze" (1970: 3).

10. For example, I remember once hearing a music student, vexed by the argument that there was in effect no such thing as musical talent, say, "Well what has Richter got, then, what is he doing, and why can't you do it?"

11. At least one musicologist, however, has argued that the significance of musical talent increased greatly as the dominant position of court patronage of the arts gave way to the public concerts of the rising middle class at the end of the eighteenth century (Raynor 1976: 14). Similarly, Sennett and Cobb (1973: 62) point out that talent originally was viewed as the opposite of inherited

position, that the availability of professional positions in terms of talent was a liberation from the earlier feudalistic system of determining profession and status strictly in terms of family position. Thus "talent" can be seen as a direct function of the emergence of political democracy.

12. Talent and comparable "badges of ability" are presented by Sennett and Cobb (1973) as a primary means of legitimizing authority in a class society. Their analysis focuses on the psychological separating of the self, the person, or the "I" from the successfully performing individual. Promotions and academic successes *happen to* working-class people; they are experienced in the passive voice: "the person disappears when the individual stands out" (1973: 195). This is quite different from experiencing success and power as the result of a talented self. Thus "talent" is not only an idiom of distinguishing individuals, but also one of class or group differentiation.

## CHAPTER FOUR

1. I myself was occasionally called on by Mr. Goldmann in this way.

2. However, it might be successfully argued that compositions are by nature neither sounding not silent, but rather are, as abstractions, logically removed from the acoustical domain of both sound and silence.

3. Such a conception of musical structure is consistent with Giddens' (1979) concept of "structuration."

## CHAPTER FIVE

1. A similar issue pertains to the word *practise*, which in sociological and anthropological discourse (where it derives from the Marxian notion of *praxis*) refers generically to the carrying out of social activity, while conservatory musicians use the word as a synonym for "rehearse," in the sense meaning preparatory training for future musical activity. Most of the evaluative concepts and categories that are at issue in concerts and recitals are largely the same as those noted in Marcus Goldmann's chamber music class. The notions of performance, rendition, and practise form a continuum of overlapping categories, and distinctions among them are made by musicians with regard to social context or frame.

2. Associated Press, *The Boston Globe*, May 1, 1981.

3. There is, of course, a sense in which "ritual" is more or less synonymous with "routine." Thus someone might refer to his "morning ritual" of brushing teeth, making coffee, and reading the newspaper. This is not the sense of the word being stressed in the present analysis.

4. In this, the opposition between what Durkheim called the "cult of the individual" and what Sennett and Cobb called the "hidden injury of class" can be seen in striking relief. The representation of a radical schism between individual and group is the precise opposite of an assimilation of the "self" to group or class experience (Sennett and Cobb 1973: 36, Durkheim 1965 [1915]: 472, cf. also my Chapter Three).

## CHAPTER SIX

1. I am obliged to Robert Hefner for many rewarding and stimulating discussions of this and many other points pertaining to problems of meaning and culture.

2. Richard Dyer, *The Boston Globe*, April 26, 1983.

3. For a brief discussion of the scholarly aspects of Cortot's pianism, see Schonberg (1963: 381–383).

4. Cicourel, for example, is quite right in saying that in many cases "the social analyst's use of abstract theoretical concepts like role actually masks the inductive or interpretive procedures whereby the actor produces behavioural displays which others and the observer label 'role behaviour.' Without a model of the actor that specifies such procedures or rules, we cannot reveal how behavioural displays are recognized as 'role taking' or 'role making' " (Cicourel 1974: 27). On the other hand, I would hope that my preceding discussions of "talented" music students and illustrious performer/teachers have provided at least the beginnings of the "model of the actor" called for by Cicourel.

5. Simon Frith specifies William Mann's 1963 column on the Beatles in *The* (London) *Times* as the first newspaper review of rock music. The incongruity of "classical" music criticism (which at the time was coterminous with music criticism) to rock music can be seen in Mann's reportorial vocabulary, which includes references to "the Beatle Quartet" and their "pandiatonic clusters," "flat submediant key switches," and "aeolian" cadences (Frith 1981: 168, *The Times*, December 27, 1963).

6. A similar point can be made in obverse form, by comparing David McAllester's report on the Navaho with W. D. Allen's comment regarding music scholars of seventeenth-century Europe. Thus, "a 'fact' in the Navaho universe is that music is not a general category of activity but has to be divided into specific aspects or kinds of music" (McAllester 1954: 4). Similarly, "for Praetorius, like most of his contemporaries, there was no such thing as *one art of music*" (Allen 1962: 11, emphasis original).

7. Lest it be thought that it is I and not Hanslick who is playing with words, Hanslick states: "The player has the privilege of venting directly

through his instrument the feeling by which he is swayed at the time, and to breathe into his performance passionate excitement, ardent longing, buoyant strength, and joy . . . his subjectiveness thus makes itself directly heard in the music, and is not merely a silent prompter" (Hanslick 1957: 76).

8. Compare Althusser and Balibar (1979), Ollman (1968), Karp and Maynard (1983). Regarding the cultural significance of metaphorical diction in everyday communication, see Whorf (1956: 134–159), Lakoff and Johnson (1980).

9. In this connection it is significant that many languages are lacking a word that is equivalent to our term *music*. For example, to the best of my knowledge there is no indigenous word for music in the languages of Africa, Aboriginal Papua New Guinea, or the Native Americans (Gourlay 1978: 16f. Keil 1979: 27–29, Nettl 1983: 20, Robertson-deCarbo 1976: 39). The idea that music is a worldwide or "universal" phenomenon is obviously premised on the assumption that the phenomenon of music can exist even where the concept *music* does not, and for the most part, ethnomusicologists have assumed exactly this. For example, in reporting on his research among the Navaho, David McAllester generated some rather clumsy phraseology in contending with the fact that the Navaho have no word for music: "A fact-finding question such as, 'What kinds of musical instruments do you use?' . . . had to be phrased, "Some people beat a drum when they sing; what other things are used like that?' " (McAllester 1954: 4). Even McAllester's tenaciously convoluted question, however, may not have completely solved the problem of cultural bias, since the "like that" in the passage just quoted neither provides nor determines—but only assumes—a Navaho criterion for distinguishing music from nonmusic. Although ethnomusicologists have often felt responsible for "correcting" biased, ethnocentric beliefs that certain non-western peoples do not make music (e.g., Nettl 1983: 15–19), my own view is that it may be just as ethnocentric to insist that the phenomenon of music can be assumed to exist even among people who have no such concept. To be sure, there have been some warnings (Gourlay 1978, Robertson-deCarbo 1976) that "music" may be a procrustean and inappropriate category when used in non-Western contexts.

# REFERENCES CITED

Adams, Richard Newbold. 1975. Energy and Structure: A Theory of Social Power. Austin: University of Texas Press.

Adler, Judith E. 1979. Artists in Offices: An Ethnography of an Academic Arts Scene. New Brunswick. N.J.: Transaction Books.

Allen, Warren Dwight. 1962. Philosophies of Music History: A Study of General Histories of Music 1600–1960. New York: Dover Publications.

Althusser, Louis, and Etienne Balibar. 1979. Reading Capital. London: Verso Editions.

Attali, Jacques. 1985. Noise: The Political Economy of Music. Minneapolis: University of Minnesota Press.

Austin, J. L. 1962. How to Do Things with Words. Cambridge: Harvard University Press.

Bauman, Richard. 1977. Verbal Art as Performance. Rowley, Mass. Newbury House Publishers.

Beattie, John. 1964. Other Cultures: Aims, Methods, and Achievements in Social Anthropology. New York: Free Press.

Becker, Howard. 1974. Art as Collective Action. *American Sociological Review* 39: 767–776.

———. 1982. Art Worlds. Berkeley: University of California Press.

Benedict, Ruth. 1951. Patterns of Culture. New York: Mentor Books.

Blacking, John. 1973. How Musical is Man? Seattle: University of Washington Press.

Blok, Anton. 1974. The Mafia of a Sicilian Village, 1860–1960: A Study of Violent Peasant Entrepreneurs. New York: Harper and Row.

Blum, Steven. 1984. Ideas of Absolute Music and the Development of Ethnomusicological Thought. Paper presented at 1984 meeting of the Society for Ethnomusicology.

Boissevain, Jeremy. 1966. Patronage in Sicily. *Man* n.s.1:18–33.

Bourdieu, Pierre. 1977. Outline of a Theory of Practice. Cambridge: Cambridge University Press.

Bridges, Doreen. 1965. Music Aptitude Tests—A Commentary. Musicology 2:53–59.

Briggs, Jean. 1970. Never in Anger: Portrait of an Eskimo Family. Cambridge: Harvard University Press.

Cage, John. 1961. Silence: Lectures and Writings. Middletown, Conn.: Wesleyan University Press.

Campbell, J. K. 1964. Honor, Family, and Patronage: A Study of Institutions and Moral Values in a Greek Mountain Community. Oxford: Clarendon Press.

Cicourel, Aaron V. 1974. Cognitive Sociology: Language and Meaning in Social Interaction. New York: The Free Press.

Cone, Edward T. 1967. Musical Structure and Musical Performance. New York: W. W. Norton.

Cooke, Deryck. 1959. The Language of Music. Oxford: Oxford University Press.

Copland, Aaron. 1957. What to Listen for in Music. New York: McGraw-Hill.

Critchley, M., and R. A. Henson. 1977. Music and the Brain. London: William Heinemann Medical Books.

Dalhaus, Carl. 1978. Die Idee der absoluten Musik. Kassel: Barenreiter.

de Man, Paul. 1978. The Epistemology of Metaphor. *Critical Inquiry* 5(1):13–30.

Douglas, Mary. 1978. Implicit Meanings: Essays in Anthropology. London: Routledge and Kegan Paul.

Durkheim, Emile. 1938. The Rules of Sociological Method. New York: The Free Press.

———. 1965 (1915). The Elementary Forms of the Religious Life. New York: The Free Press.

Evans-Pritchard, E. E. 1940. The Nuer. Oxford: Clarendon Press.

———. 1956. Nuer Religion. Oxford: Oxford University Press.

Faulkner, Robert. 1971. Hollywood Studio Musicians. Chicago: Aldine Atherton.

———. 1973. Orchestra Interaction: Some Features of Communication and Authority in an Artistic Organization. *Sociological Quarterly* 14: 147–157.

Feld, Steven. 1984. Sound Structure as Social Structure. *Ethnomusicology* 28: 383–409.

Fortes, Meyer. 1945. The Dynamics of Clanship among the Tallensi. Oxford: Oxford University Press.

———. 1949. The Web of Kinship among the Tallensi. Oxford: Oxford University Press.

Frith, Simon. 1981. Sound Effects. New York: Pantheon.

Garfinkel, Harold. 1967. Studies in Ethnomethodology. Englewood Cliffs, N.J.: Prentice-Hall.

Geertz, Clifford. 1973. The Interpretation of Cultures. New York: Basic Books.
————. 1976. "From the Native's Point of View": On the Nature of Anthropological Understanding. *In* Keith H. Basso and Henry Selby (eds.): Meaning in Anthropology, Albuquerque: University of New Mexico Press, pp. 221–237.
————. 1983. Local Knowledge. New York: Basic Books.
Giddens, Anthony. 1976. New Rules of Sociological Method. New York: Basic Books.
————. 1977. Studies in Social and Political Theory. New York: Basic Books.
————. 1979. Central Problems in Social Theory. Berkeley: University of California Press.
Goffman, Erving. 1967. Interaction Ritual: Essays on Face-to-Face Behavior. Garden City, N.Y.: Anchor Books.
————. 1971. Relations in Public. New York: Harper Colophon.
————. 1974. Frame Analysis: An Essay on the Organization of Experience. New York: Harper Colophon.
Gourlay, K. A. 1978. Towards a Reassessment of the Ethnomusicologist's Role in Research. *Ethnomusicology* 22:1–35.
Hanslick, Eduard. 1957 (1891). The Beautiful in Music. Indianapolis: Bobbs Merrill.
Herndon, Marcia, and Norma McLeod. 1979. Music as Culture. Norwood, Pa: Norwood Editions.
Herzfeld, Michael. 1984. The Significance of the Insignificant: Blasphemy as Ideology. *Man* n.s. 19: 653–664.
Holy, Ladislav, and Milan Stuchlik, editors. 1981. The Structure of Folk Models. New York: Academic Press.
Ives, Charles E. 1962. Essays before a Sonata. *In* Claude Debussy, Charles E. Ives, and Ferruccio Busoni: Three Classics in the Aesthetic of Music. New York: Norton.
Kalmus, H., and D. B. Fry. 1980. On tune deafness (dysmelodia): frequency, development, genetics and musical background. *Annals of Human Genetics* 43: 369–382.
Karp, Ivan, and Kent Maynard. 1983. Reading *The Nuer. Current Anthropology* 24 (4): 481–503.
Keil, Charles. 1966. Urban Blues. Chicago: University of Chicago Press.
————. 1979. Tiv Song. Chicago: University of Chicago Press.
Kerman, Joseph, with Vivian Kerman. 1980. Listen. New York: Worth Publishers.
Labov, William. 1972. Language in the Inner City. Philadelphia: University of Pennsylvania Press.
Laing, R. D. 1961. Self and Others. Harmondsworth, N.J.: Penguin Books.

Lakoff, George, and Mark Johnson. 1980. Metaphors We Live By. Chicago: University of Chicago Press.

Leach, Edmund. 1977. Political Systems of Highland Burma: A Study of Kachin Social Structure. London: The Athlone Press.

Lévi-Strauss, Claude. 1969. The Raw and the Cooked. New York: Harper Torchbooks.

Lord, Albert. 1960. The Singer of Tales. Cambridge: Harvard University Press.

Lowie, Robert. 1961. Primitive Society. New York: Harper Torchbooks.

McAllester, David P. 1954. Enemy Way Music: A Study of Social and Esthetic Values as Seen in Navaho Music. Cambridge: Peabody Museum of American Archaeology and Ethnology, Harvard University.

————. 1980. Music as Culture, by Marcia Herndon and Norma McLeod. Norwood, Pa: Norwood Editions. Review in Ethnomusicology 24 (2): 305–307.

MacGaffey, Wyatt. 1980. African Religions: Types and Generalizations. In Ivan Karp and Charles S. Bird (eds.): Exploration in African Systems of Thought. Bloomington: Indiana University Press, pp. 301–328.

Machlis, Joseph. 1963. The Enjoyment of Music. New York: W. W. Norton.

Marcus, George E. 1980. Rhetoric and the Ethnographic Genre in Anthropological Research. Current Anthropology 21 (4): 507–510.

Marcus, George E., and Dick Cushman. 1982. Ethnographies as Texts. Annual Review of Anthropology 11:25–69.

Marcus, George E., and Michael M. J. Fischer. 1986. Anthropology as Cultural Critique: An Experimental Moment in the Human Sciences. Chicago: University of Chicago Press.

Marshall, Christopher. 1982. Towards a Comparative Aesthetics of Music. In Robert Falck and Timothy Rice (eds.): Cross Cultural Perspectives on Music. Toronto: University of Toronto Press.

Merriam, Alan P. 1964. The Anthropology of Music. Evanston, Ill.: Northwestern University Press.

————. 1967. The Ethnomusicology of the Flathead Indians. Chicago: Aldine.

————. 1977. Definitions of "Comparative Musicology" and "Ethnomusicology": An Historical-Theoretical Perspective. Ethnomusicology 21: 189–204.

Messenger, John. 1958. Esthetic Talent. Basic College Quarterly 4: 20–24.

Meyer, Leonard B. 1956. Emotion and Meaning in Music. Chicago: University of Chicago Press.

Nadeau, Roland, and William Tesson. 1981. Listen: A Guide to the Pleasures of Music. Dubuque, Ia: Kendall/Hunt Publishing Company.

Nattiez, Jean-Jacques. 1977. The Contribution of Musical Semiotics to the Semiotic Discussion in General. *In* Thomas Sebeok (ed.): A Profusion of Signs. Bloomington: Indiana University Press.

Nettl, Bruno. 1956. Music in Primitive Culture. Cambridge: Harvard University Press.

———. 1983. The Study of Ethnomusicology: Twenty-Nine Issues and Concepts. Urbana: University of Illinois Press.

Ollman, Bertell. 1968. Marx's Use of "Class." *American Journal of Sociology* 73: 573–580.

Ortner, Sherry B. 1984. Theory in Anthropology since the Sixties. *Comparative Studies in Society and History* 26 (1): 126–166.

Radcliffe, Philip. 1968. Beethoven's String Quartets. New York: E. P. Dutton.

Raynor, Henry. 1976. Music and Society Since 1815. New York: Schocken Books.

Rice, Timothy. 1982. From the Editor. *Ethnomusicology* 26: v.

Robertson-deCarbo, Carol. 1976. *Tayil* as Category and Communication Among the Argentine Mapuche: A Methodological Suggestion. *Yearbook of the International Folk Music Council,* 8: 35–52.

Salzer, Felix. 1962. Structural Hearing: Tonal Coherence in Music, Vol. One. New York: Dover.

Sapir, Edward. 1949. Selected Writings of Edward Sapir, edited by David Mandelbaum. Berkeley: University of California Press.

Schenker, Heinrich. 1954 (1906). Harmony. Chicago: University of Chicago Press.

Schonberg, Harold. 1963. The Great Pianists. New York: Simon and Schuster.

Sennett, Richard, and Jonathan Cobb. 1973. The Hidden Injuries of Class. New York: Vintage Books.

Shepherd, John, Phil Virden, Graham Vulliamy, and Trevor Wishart. 1977. Whose Music? A Sociology of Musical Languages. New Brunswick, N.J.: Transaction Books.

Sidran, Ben. 1971 Black Talk: How the Music of Black America Created a Radical Alternative to the Values of Western Literary Tradition. New York: Holt, Rinehart and Winston.

Smith, M. G. 1956. On Segmentary Lineage Systems. *Journal of the Royal Anthropological Institute of Great Britain and Ireland* 86: 39–80.

Spaeth, Sigmund. 1949. The Art of Enjoying Music. New York: Permabooks.

Spindler, George, and Louise Spindler. 1983. Anthropologists View American Culture. *Annual Review of Anthropology* 12: 49–78.

Sudnow, David. 1978. Ways of the Hand: The Organization of Improvised Conduct. New York: Bantam Books.

Truscott, Harold. 1968. Beethoven's Late String Quartets. London: Dobson Books.

Tylor, Edward B. 1958 (1871). The Origins of Culture. New York: Harper and Row.

Wagner, Roy. 1981. The Invention of Culture. Chicago: The University of Chicago Press.

Weatherford, J. McIver. 1981. Tribes on the Hill. New York: Rawson, Wade.

Whorf, Benjamin Lee. 1956. Language Thought and Reality, edited by John B. Carroll. Cambridge: The MIT Press.

Whyte, William Foote. 1955. Street Corner Society. Chicago: University of Chicago Press.

Williams, Raymond. 1977. Marxism and Literature. Oxford: Oxford University Press.

Wilson, Frank R. 1987. Tone Deaf and All Thumbs? An Invitation to Music Making for Late Bloomers and Non-Prodigies. New York: Viking.

Yengoyan, Aram A. 1986. Theory in Anthropology: On the Demise of the Concept of Culture. *Comparative Studies in Society and History* 28 (2): 368–374.

Zuckerkandl, Victor. 1956. Sound and Symbol: Music and the External World. Princeton: Princeton University Press.

# INDEX